COFFIN-MAKING
AND
UNDER TAKING

SPECIAL APPLIANCES; LANCASHIRE COFFINS;
SOUTHERN COUNTIES AND OTHER COFFINS;
CHILDREN'S COFFINS; ADULTS' COVERED
COFFINS; POLISHING COFFINS; INSCRIPTION
PLATES; COFFIN FURNITURE; TRIMMING
OR LINING; ORNAMENTED AND PANELLED
COFFINS; SHELLS AND OUTER COFFINS; LEAD
COFFINS; UNDERTAKING

EDITED BY

PAUL N. HASLUCK

British Library Cataloguing-in-Publication Data
A catalogue record for this book is available from the
British Library

CONTENTS

Woodworking

Woodworking is the process of making items from wood. Along with stone, mud and animal parts, wood was one of the first materials worked by early humans. There are incredibly early examples of woodwork, evidenced in Mousterian stone tools used by Neanderthal man, which demonstrate our affinity with the wooden medium. In fact, the very development of civilisation is linked to the advancement of increasingly greater degrees of skill in working with these materials.

Examples of Bronze Age wood-carving include tree trunks worked into coffins from northern Germany and Denmark and wooden folding-chairs. The site of Fellbach-Schmieden in Germany has provided fine examples of wooden animal statues from the Iron Age. Woodworking is depicted in many ancient Egyptian drawings, and a considerable amount of ancient Egyptian furniture (such as stools, chairs, tables, beds, chests) has been preserved in tombs. The inner coffins found in the tombs were also made of wood. The metal used by the Egyptians for woodworking tools was originally copper and eventually, after 2000 BC, bronze - as ironworking was unknown until much later. Historically, woodworkers relied upon the woods native to their region, until transportation and trade innovations made more exotic woods available to the craftsman.

Today, often as a contemporary artistic and 'craft' medium, wood is used both in traditional and modern styles; an excellent material for delicate as well as forceful artworks. Wood is used in forms of sculpture, trade, and decoration including chip carving, wood burning, and marquetry, offering a fascination, beauty, and complexity in the grain that often shows even when the medium is painted. It is in some ways easier to shape than harder substances, but an artist or craftsman must develop specific skills to carve it properly. 'Wood carving' is really an entire genre itself, and involves cutting wood generally with a knife in one hand, or a chisel by two hands - or, with one hand on a chisel and one hand on a mallet. The phrase may also refer to the finished product, from individual sculptures to hand-worked mouldings composing part of a tracery.

The making of sculpture in wood has been extremely widely practiced but survives much less well than the other main materials such as stone and bronze, as it is vulnerable to decay, insect damage, and fire. It therefore forms an important hidden element in the arts and crafts history of many cultures. Outdoor wood sculptures do not last long in most parts of the world, so that we have little idea how the totem pole tradition developed. Many of the most important sculptures of China and Japan in particular are in wood, and the great majority of African sculptures and that of Oceania also use this medium. There are various forms of carving which can be utilised; 'chip carving' (a style of carving in which knives or chisels are used to remove small chips of the material), 'relief carving' (where figures are carved in a flat panel of wood), 'Scandinavian flat-plane' (where figures are carved in large flat planes, created primarily using a carving knife - and rarely rounded or sanded afterwards) and 'whittling' (simply carving shapes using just a knife). Each of these techniques will need slightly varying tools, but broadly speaking, a specialised 'carving knife' is essential, alongside a 'gouge' (a tool with a curved cutting edge used in a variety of forms and sizes for carving hollows, rounds and sweeping curves), a 'chisel' and a 'coping saw' (a small saw, used to cut off chunks of wood at once).

Wood turning is another common form of woodworking, used to create wooden objects on a lathe. Woodturning differs from most other forms of woodworking in that the wood is moving while a stationary tool is used to cut and shape it. There are two distinct methods of turning wood: 'spindle turning' and 'bowl' or 'faceplate turning'. Their key difference is in the orientation of the wood grain, relative to the axis of the lathe. This variation in orientation changes the tools and techniques used. In spindle turning, the grain runs lengthways along the lathe bed, as if a log was mounted in the lathe. Grain is thus always perpendicular to the direction of rotation under the tool. In bowl turning, the grain runs at right angles to the axis, as if a plank were mounted across the chuck. When a bowl blank rotates, the angle that the grain makes with the cutting tool continually changes between the easy cuts of lengthways and downwards across the grain to two places per rotation where the tool is cutting across the grain and even upwards across it. This varying grain angle limits some of the tools that may be used and requires additional skill in order to cope with it.

The origin of woodturning dates to around 1300 BC when the Egyptians first developed a two-person lathe. One person would turn the wood with a rope while the other used a sharp tool to cut shapes in the wood. The Romans improved the Egyptian design with the addition of a turning bow. Early bow lathes were also developed and used in Germany, France and Britain. In the Middle Ages a pedal replaced hand-operated turning, freeing both the craftsman's hands to hold the woodturning tools. The pedal was usually connected to a pole, often a straight-grained sapling. The system today is called the 'spring pole' lathe. Alternatively, a two-person lathe, called a 'great lathe', allowed a piece to turn continuously (like today's power lathes). A master would cut the wood while an apprentice turned the crank.

As an interesting aside, the term 'bodger' stems from pole

lathe turners who used to make chair legs and spindles. A bodger would typically purchase all the trees on a plot of land, set up camp on the plot, and then fell the trees and turn the wood. The spindles and legs that were produced were sold in bulk, for pence per dozen. The bodger's job was considered unfinished because he only made component parts. The term now describes a person who leaves a job unfinished, or does it badly. This could not be more different from perceptions of modern carpentry; a highly skilled trade in which work involves the construction of buildings, ships, timber bridges and concrete framework. The word 'carpenter' is the English rendering of the Old French word *carpentier* (later, *charpentier*) which is derived from the Latin *carpentrius;* '(maker) of a carriage.' Carpenters traditionally worked with natural wood and did the rougher work such as framing, but today many other materials are also used and sometimes the finer trades of cabinet-making and furniture building are considered carpentry.

As is evident from this brief historical and practical overview of woodwork, it is an incredibly varied and exciting genre of arts and crafts; an ancient tradition still relevant in the modern day. Woodworkers range from hobbyists, individuals operating from the home environment, to artisan professionals with specialist workshops, and eventually large-scale factory operations. We hope the reader is inspired by this book to create some woodwork of their own.

COFFIN-MAKING AND UNDERTAKING

CHAPTER I

SPECIAL APPLIANCES; LANCASHIRE COFFINS.

UNDERTAKING is a business which, especially in country districts, may with advantage be allied to that of the builder, wheelwright, or cabinetmaker, the necessary experience, except in a few extra details, being very similar to that requisite in all branches of woodworking. Undertaking may be interpreted not only as coffin making, but as including the management of funerals throughout.

This book will show how to make coffins by the Lancashire method, and also in the style adopted in the South of England. For making coffins in the Lancashire style, some special appliances are necessary. One of these is the cramp (Fig. 1), which has two wooden sides A, 33 in. long and 2 1/2 in. square. Screws B are fitted to these at about 6 in. from each end, thus leaving a space of 21 in. between. The screws are continued at one end to form winch handles, as shown at C, the bar being drilled through at about 2 in. from the winch to receive a pin; iron washers are screwed to one of the side pieces for this pin to work against. To the other cheek, nuts to fit the screws must be fixed, as at D, and the screws should be long enough to allow the sides to open 3 ft. in the clear, and should be threaded sufficiently to close them to within about 16 in. The cramp will then answer for any size of adult coffin.

The breast-board, another useful article, is shown by Figs. 2 and 3. It is made of four boards about 18 in. long, 4 1/2in. by 1in. (or two 9 -in. boards would do). These are fixed together in pairs by the ledges F, which are about 17 in. long and are nailed on so that they overhang two of the boards E half their length. The overhanging parts are slotted to within an inch of the right-hand boards, and also of their ends, and bolts fitted with wing nuts are put through each of the loose boards, as at G. These pass through the slots in the ledges, by means of which the breast-board can be made of any width from 18 in. to 2 ft.

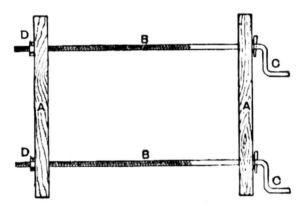

Fig. 1.—Cramp for Bending Sides of Coffin.

An iron cramp for the head of a coffin is another special appliance required; it is shown in Fig. 4, and is made of 1/2-in. bar iron with the end H bent downwards for about 2 in., and the other end threaded for a length of about 4 in. and fitted with a wing nut K. The full length of the straight part is 13 in., and it is fitted with a sliding bracket piece I.

The remaining tools required, with the exception of the measuring rule, will be found in the carpenter's ordinary kit. The common 2-ft. rule would serve the purpose; but two 1-in. by 1/4-in. laths, about 3 ft. 3 in. long, fastened together with a screw at one end, will be found to answer the purpose far better. It can be opened out and laid on the body, and the proper length marked on it. In taking measurements for a coffin, it is usual to allow 2 in. in length and 1 in. in width, and if both these are marked direct on the rule, mistakes will not be likely to arise. Length, and width at shoulders, as a rule, are the only measurements required, except in special cases, which, readily recognised, can be provided for accordingly.

At the time of taking the measurements, all particulars as to name and age, date of death, etc., for the inscription on the coffin plate should be obtained, and their accuracy carefully verified.

Fig. 2.

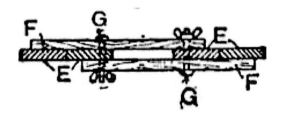

Fig. 3.

Figs. 2 and 3.—Plan and Section of Breast-board.

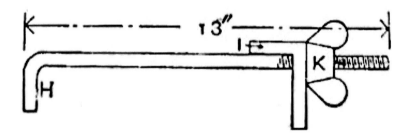

Fig.4.—Iron Cramp For Head of Coffin.

Fig. 5 and 6 show the scales for coffins both taper and parallel, ranging from 2 ft. 9 in. long to full size. "Full size" means any size beyond 5 ft. 6 in. long. The list given at the head of the next page applies to taper coffins.

Two scales, as shown in Figs. 5 and 6, should be made. These can be drawn half size on a piece of board, when the necessary sizes and widths of the various parts can be seen at a glance.

Whilst the length of a coffin and its width at the breast almost always correspond to the measurements taken (the former usually regulating, the depth and width of head and foot), no hard-and-fast rule can be given, and in some cases it may be necessary to take the measurement for the depth also, whilst in others the width at breast may be such as to require the width at head and foot, as well as the depth, to be full size, whilst in length it will be much shorter.

LENGTH OF BOTTOM.		WIDTH OF BOTTOM.		HEIGHT OF SIDES.	
Size.		Head.	Foot.	Head.	Foot.
	ft. in.	in.	in.	in.	in.
1	2 9	$5\frac{1}{8}$	$3\frac{3}{4}$	$8\frac{1}{2}$	$7\frac{1}{4}$
2	3 0	$5\frac{3}{4}$	$4\frac{1}{4}$	9	$7\frac{5}{8}$
3	3 3	$6\frac{3}{8}$	$4\frac{3}{4}$	$9\frac{1}{2}$	8
4	3 6	7	$5\frac{1}{4}$	10	$8\frac{3}{4}$
5	3 9	$7\frac{5}{8}$	$5\frac{7}{8}$	$10\frac{1}{2}$	$8\frac{7}{8}$
6	4 0	$8\frac{1}{4}$	$6\frac{1}{2}$	11	$9\frac{1}{8}$
7	4 3	$8\frac{7}{8}$	7	$11\frac{1}{2}$	$9\frac{1}{2}$
8	4 6	$9\frac{1}{2}$	$7\frac{5}{8}$	12	10
9	4 9	$10\frac{1}{8}$	$8\frac{1}{4}$	$12\frac{1}{2}$	$10\frac{3}{8}$
10	5 0	$10\frac{3}{4}$	$8\frac{3}{4}$	13	11
11	5 3	$11\frac{3}{8}$	$9\frac{3}{4}$	$13\frac{1}{2}$	$11\frac{1}{2}$
12	5 6	12	10	14	12

The scale for parallel coffins can be founded upon that given above, beginning with the smallest size for all measurements, and ranging them in proportion up to full size or the maximum measurements given—namely, 8 in. wide at head, 7 in. at foot, and the sides 12 in. deep. These should be sufficient to enable anyone to make coffins in proportion.

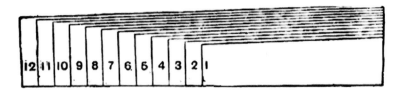

Fig. 5.—Scale of Coffin Sides.

In making a Lancashire coffin, the first thing is to set out the bottom. Although this, not being seen, need not be of the same wood as the other parts, it must be sound, and should be in one piece if possible; but if, as sometimes happens, there are no boards in stock wide enough (and it is not generally economical to use for bottoms boards that will make good lids), the bottom must be jointed, and if this is done properly there will be no sacrifice of strength; but the time consumed in making the joints must be considered in calculating the cost. In all cases where the board is too narrow by more than an inch, a piece should be put on at each side instead of at one side only. The fact that the former means will involve a smaller length of jointing will be appreciated, perhaps, by reference to Fig. 7. If the widening pieces are more than 1 in. wide they should be nailed at their ends to fix them in position, and a few 1/4-in. holes can be bored right through them into the board to a depth of 2 in.; into these holes well-glued dowels can be driven. This plan, illustrated in Fig. 7, is far better than nailing, and takes but very little longer. This joint will not yield and crack the pitch—an inevitable occurrence if the extra width required is made up by nailing a piece on one side only; in which case the coffin might almost as well not be pitched at all, the weight of the body being well-nigh certain to break the joint.

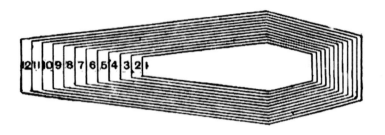

Fig. 6.—Scale of Coffin Bottoms.

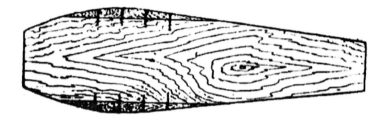

Fig. 7.—Bottom Board Spliced.

In Lancashire, common coffins are usually made of pitch pine, and the better ones of oak (usually American); while in the southern counties the common ones are of elm and the best of English oak. For Lancashire coffins, the boards required are—one for the bottom and one for the lid, each 3/4 in. thick, and of the requisite width; one each for head and foot, 8 in. and 7 in. respectively, and both about 14 in. long by 3/4 in. or 1 in. thick; and two sides, 6 ft. 6 in. long, 12 in. wide by 1/2 in. thick.

Take the board selected for the bottom, make a line L (Fig. 8) up its centre; from this, square across the head at M, about 2 in. from the end; then, at the proper distance for the length of coffin required, square the foot N, and at 18 in. from the head mark the breast-line o; lastly, mark the two other lines shown parallel with the breast, and 4 in. on each side of it. The width of the head, 8 in., and of the foot, 7 in., can be marked off on the head and foot lines, half on each side of the centre line; also the width at the breast can be marked—not on the breast line, but on the line nearer the head.

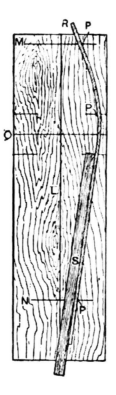

Fig. 8.—Setting Out Bottom of Coffin.

A wire nail is now driven in at each of the points where the above marks intersect (see P, Fig. 8), and a thin rod of wood bent round the nails, inside the two end ones and outside the middle one, gives a continuous curve from head to foot, which must be corrected by applying a straightedge inside the rod, with one end at the 4-in. mark nearest the foot, as shown in Fig. 8. The rod being pressed against the straightedge as illustrated, and kept to the three nails, a pencil mark can be run round the outside of the rod to give the proper shape. The other side can be struck in the same way.

Fig. 9.—Bottom of Coffin Fixed on Bench.

The bottom can now be cut out, following the curved lines, and the edges should be roughly planed; but the ends must not be cut off until the coffin is put together. The head and foot will require planing on one side, and one end is squared and cut off. Two nails are driven into each of the head and foot marks on the bottom. and then the head and foot are stood upright on the bench, squared ends uppermost; the bottom is laid on them, keeping the head and foot close up to, but outside, the nails in the marks; the bottom is now nailed to them.

When both head and foot are secured, the guide nails can be withdrawn, and the bottom placed in the bench-vice, with the head and foot resting firmly on the bench, as shown in Fig. 9; and while in this position the side edges of the head and foot are planed off level with the bottom, from which the proper bevel will be obtained.

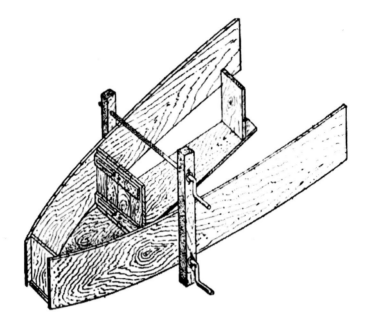

Fig. 10.—Method of Bending Coffin Sides.

The sides are put on whilst the bottom is on the bench. One side is nailed to it at the head end as far as the nails will pull it sufficiently close, and it is also nailed to the head itself, taking care to keep the latter square with the bottom. The other side having been treated in the same way, the coffin can be removed from the bench and turned up on its bottom, with the head resting on a trestle and the foot on the floor. The iron cramp (Fig. 4, p. 11) may now be fixed across the top of the head to keep the sides from springing off during the process of bending. Fix the breast-board (Fig. 2, p. 11) inside the coffin on the breast line, adjusting it to the width of the bottom at that point; and, lastly, place the cramp (Fig. 1, p. 10) about a foot beyond the breast-board, allowing the bottom of the coffin to rest on the bottom screw (see Fig. 10).

The coffin is now taken into the open air, and the head end filled loosely with shavings, a few also being put the other side of the breast-board. The shavings are then set on fire, and as the heat takes effect the screws of the cramp are gradually tightened up until the sides fit close to the bottom and breast-board, when they are nailed firmly to the bottom and the foot. If the sides or breast-board seem in danger of catching fire, as they are apt to do if the sides are very stubborn, water should be sprinkled over them with a brush. After the sides are firmly nailed, the cramps, etc., can be removed, and the projecting ends of the sides and bottom cut level and cleaned off with the plane. Then the entire coffin may be finished off with the scraper and glasspaper.

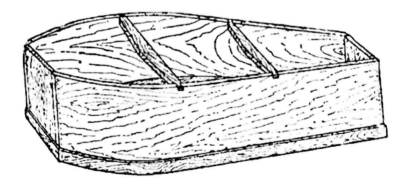

Fig. 11.—Body of Coffin.

The plinth is about 2 1/4 in. by 1/2 in., with the top edge bevelled, and should be fixed to the head and foot first, and the ends cleaned off straight with the sides of the coffin, so that the sides will bed fair on them. In fixing the sides, nail the head end first, gradually bending them round and finishing at the foot. When preparing the plinth, always leave it quite as thick at the top edge as at the bottom, thus ensuring a good fit where the work will be observable.

Cross pieces, as shown in Fig. 11, are necessary to stiffen the sides, and are also useful to straighten them if the sides should happen to get pulled out of shape; but providing the sides are straight, and the coffin is comparatively short, one cross piece will be sufficient, and should be placed about midway of the length of the coffin, unless there is any special reason for placing it elsewhere, when it can be moved a few inches nearer the foot, but not nearer the breast, that being already the strongest part. These cross pieces are usually made from the waste cut off the bottom or lid, and in shape as shown in Fig. 11, probably because the waste pieces make that shape most conveniently. They are fixed by dovetailing to the sides (see Fig. 12), and should fit sufficiently tightly to allow of their being knocked out by the hand. Whilst the length of these cross pieces is being taken, the sides of the coffin should be pressed out or in as required, so as to make them straight when the cross pieces are in position, and they should be let into the sides deeply enough for the lid to be about 1/8 in.

above them, so as to allow for the lining, which will fill up the slot to a certain extent.

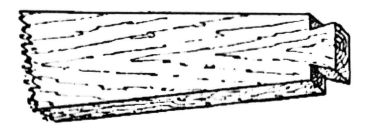

Fig. 12.—Dovetail on Cross Piece.

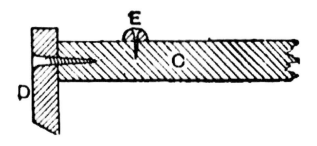

Fig. 13.—Section of Lid Showing Rim and Bead.

In making the lid, lay the selected board on top of the coffin, best side uppermost, and in such a position that all blemishes will be cut off in the waste wood, then mark it round underneath, keeping the pencil flat against the sides and ends of the coffin. Cut round outside these marks, and plane the edges until the marks are removed, at the same time squaring all edges. Plane the top, and, if necessary, scrape it ready for polishing. It should now project evenly about 1/12 in. all round the coffin, and be ready for the rim D, which is made of the section shown in Fig. 13, about 2 in. by 1/2 in.

For fixing the rim round the lid, the same procedure may be followed as with the plinth, first putting on the end pieces, then planing the ends square to receive the sides.

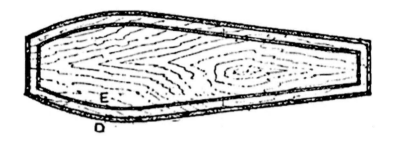

Fig. 14—lid of coffin

As shown in Fig. 13, the rim projects 1/4 in. above the lid C, and the best way to get this projection even is to use a small piece of wood of that thickness as a gauge. A bead E, 7/16 in. wide and 1/4 in. thick, is added inside the trim. To fix the bead make a small block 1 1/4 in. wide, and, starting with one of the side beads, fix it as close to the end as possible, so as to be clear of the mitre; then place the block between the rim and the bead, and gradually force it along an inch or two at the time, nailing the bead at every place. After the two side beads are on, the end pieces are laid across them and the mitres marked and cut with a chisel.

The lid, as seen from above, will now present the

appearance shown in Fig. 14, and should fit the coffin easily but closely.

The next thing in practice is to polish the coffin, but as this operation will be described later it may be passed over for the present. Meanwhile the furniture can be put on. In Fig. 15 is shown one end of the coffin, with rings inserted; this may seem a curious idea to some, as in many parts it is usual to put a plate and handle on the head and foot similar to those on the sides; but the rings, being stronger, are more suitable for this style of coffin; and if plates had to be used, they would either be very small in size, or the head and foot would have to be made wider.

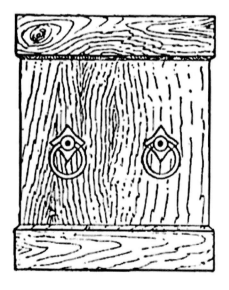

Fig. 15.—Rings on End of Coffin.

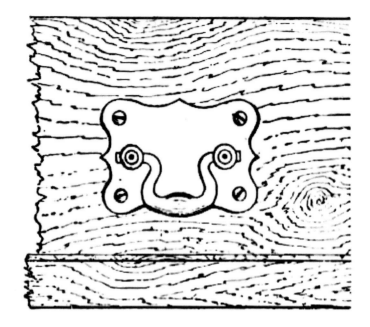

Fig. 16.—Handle and Plate on Side of Coffin.

The rings are put in midway as regards the height when the lid is on, and are distant from the sides a quarter of the width of the head or foot. For instance, the foot being 8 in. wide, the hole for the shank of the ring will be bored 2 in. from the corner.

Fig. 16 shows part of the side of the coffin, showing in position one of the three plates required for each side, the outer ones about 7 in. clear from each end, and the central one midway between, and they must be fixed in the same position as regards height as the rings on the ends, and care should be taken to get them all in a straight line one with another, and parallel with the plinth.

When the plates are fixed, the handles can be put on, the holes in the plates showing where to bore the necessary holes for the bosses in which the handles swing. Those shown in the figure are the old-fashioned kind, in which the shank is split so that it can be opened out and clenched inside; in Chapter V. better kinds of furniture are shown.

The next thing is to pitch the coffin, and this should never on any account be omitted. The best Swedish pitch should be used because it is tougher than that made at gasworks, and not so liable to crack. All crevices should be puttied up, and if there are any loose knots or faulty places in the bottom of the coffin a piece of brown paper should be tacked over them. The pitch having been heated to boiling point, pour in a good lot at the breast, and guide it along the joint towards the foot, up the joint of foot and side, down again, across the foot, and up the other side, then back along the other side of the bottom, and up the joints of head in the same way as at the foot; then, turning the coffin on its bottom on a pair of trestles, pour some pitch on the faulty places, brown paper, etc., if any, and cover it well with a mop made by wrapping some calico round a strip of wood. The clinches of the handle fasteners should also be well covered with pitch in the same way.

Pitched as above, the coffin will be watertight and perfectly safe; and since the cost of making it so will not be more than a shilling, there is really no excuse for neglecting it.

The coffin is now ready for the lining, but before detailing how this is done it may be well to describe the method of making a coffin of the southern pattern, and then to show the various methods of lining or trimming both kinds.

CHAPTER II

SOUTHERN COUNTIES AND OTHER COFFINS

COFFINS of the southern counties style will doubtless be thought the best in some parts of the country: they certainly possess the advantage over others that their making does not necessitate the use of special tools.

The bottom of a southern pattern coffin is set out as in Fig. 17. First draw a line A up the middle of the board, and from this square off the head and foot lines B and C, and at 18 in. from the head square off the breast line D; then, at equal distances each side of the centre line, set off the widths of the breast, head, and foot, the two latter dimensions, for a full-sized coffin, being 12 in. and 10 in. respectively. Connect these points by pencil and straightedge, and cut out the bottom, taking care to keep just outside the lines; and in cutting the ends (which in this case have to be cut off) the saw should be held out of the upright, so that it undercuts about

1/12 in. to give the necessary bevel to the head and foot, this style of coffin being made about 2 in. longer at the top than the bottom, for which reason the bottom need be made only about 1 in. longer than the body. The un-evenness left by the saw should be roughly planed off, and the sharp corner at the breast line can be removed at the same time, making an easy curve for a length of about 2 in. Sometimes the curve is made 5 in. or 6 in. long, the side of the smoothing plane being used as a template.

The ends and sides can now be prepared. The ends are 15 in. and 13 in. long for the head and foot respectively. The bottom gives the widths. The sides are usually cut 6 ft. 6 in. long, 14 in. wide at the head, and 12 in. at the foot, the whole, including the lid, being 3/4 in. in thickness, this being strong enough for ordinary cases, although 1 in. looks better.

In some cases, where the coffin is for a very slight person, the sides may be 1 in. less in width, and if the coffin is very narrow at the breast—say, less than 17 in.—the head and foot had better be reduced as well; but sufficient width must be allowed for the head- and foot-plates. Should the coffin be very wide at the breast—say, anything over 22 in.—the head and foot may be 1/2 in. wider than the dimensions given above; but these are very exceptional cases, and, generally speaking, the standard measurement for head and foot (12 in. and 10 in. respectively) should not be departed from.

The most suitable material for common coffins is elm,

which looks well when simply oiled, and is cheap; but for good coffins oak is the best, though more expensive, and also requires more work to bring it to a good surface.

The ends need be planed on one side only, and, leaving the edges as they come from the saw, they can both be squared across on the rough side, and a couple of nails driven in as guides. The bottom is then laid flat on the bench, marked side uppermost, and one end packed up with a piece of wood laid across the bench. The head or foot is then placed against the end of bottom, with the nails resting on the inside, and is then nailed to the bottom; and if the bottom was cut at the proper angle, the ends will spread about 1 in., although 1/4 in. more will not matter.

When both the head and foot are nailed on, the edges can be planed off level with the edges of the bottom ready for the sides, and the sides can be prepared. These must be paired, and a face mark put on the inside bottom edge (this is important, as, if put on anywhere else, it gets planed off). The sides are planed up on the outside, and at the ends only on the inside, where they will fit the head and foot. Both edges also must be planed quite straight, and both sides, when finished, must be the same width at each end.

The bottom of the coffin can now be held in the vice, as shown by Fig. 9, p. 15, and after the breast marks have been squared over the edges and marked on the bottom, one of the sides can be laid on, allowing plenty of length at both head and foot, and the breast line marked. This will be for the middle saw kerf (necessary for building), and as it is usual to make five, set off two more lines on each side of it at 1/2-in. intervals. For a long curve the kerfs may be 1 in. or more apart.

Transfer these marks to the other one, and square them across on the inside from the bottom or face edges. They can then be cut in of even depth, using a fine sharp saw, to within about 3/16 in. of the planed side. The best way is to gauge on that distance from the planed side on each edge, and cut just down to the gauge marks. Part of a side is shown in Fig. 18 with the saw kerfs made, and Figs. 19 and 20 show top views of the edges with the kerfs made in different ways. The former, with the kerfs square with face of board, is the one recommended; but the other is shown, as it is largely used in some parts.

The saw kerfs having been damped with boiling water to ensure easy bending, the sides are ready for nailing on, and holes should be punched with a bradawl within 1/4 in. of the bottom edge, at about 4-in. intervals, allowing 1/2 in. on either side of the saw kerfs. With the middle saw kerf on the breast mark and the edges level with the bottom, all the nails can be put in on the head end past the saw kerfs, and the side can be nailed across the end to the head, first trying the angle the head makes with the bottom. The foot end of the side can then be pressed down gently and nailed to the bottom, and then to the foot, after which the coffin is turned over and the other side put on in the same way. Care must be taken to keep the middle saw kerf to the breast line, as if this is not done, the top of the coffin will be lopsided.

Fig. 17.—Board Marked Out for Coffin Bottom.

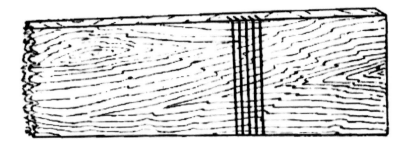

Fig. 18.—Part of Coffin Side with Saw Kerfs.

Fig. 19.—Saw Kerfs Square with Face of Side.

Fig. 20.—Saw Kerfs Cut Fan Shape.

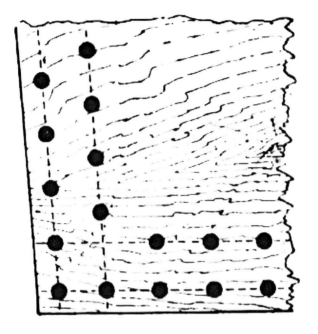

Fig. 21.—Method of Nailing

The projecting ends of the sides are to be cut off level with the head and foot, also the ends of the latter level with the bottom, and smoothed with the plane.

It is as well to leave the top of the head and foot slightly rounding in the width—about 1/16 in. high in the middle is sufficient—the reason for which is to cause the lid to fit tightly without the necessity of putting a screw in the end grain.

The coffin is now ready for the lid. This should be laid on the top, and have its outline marked as before described; but in sawing it out, keep well outside the marks, and in cutting across the head and foot hold the saw the reverse way from when cutting out the bottom. When the lid is sawn to shape, it must be planed on the top, and also underneath round the edge for about 1 1/2 in Place the lid on the coffin with an even margin all round, and bore holes through the lid at fully 5/8 in. from the sides and 5 3/4 in. from the ends, and with an ordinary 1 1/2-in. screw fix the lid temporarily, and plane the lid all round, so that it shows an equal projection over sides and ends, keeping the latter of the same bevel as the head and foot. This done, the lid may be removed, and gauge marks made as guides for nailing. Set a gauge to 5/8 in. and one to 2 in., and run them all round lightly along the top and bottom and up each end of the sides and ends of the coffin, and all round the lid. Then set a pair of compasses to the width between the gauge lines (1 3/8 in.), and, starting at the foot end of coffin, mark along each of the outside gauge marks, regulating the few last spaces towards the end in each case, as well as all the short lengths at head and foot, by increasing or reducing the distance, so as to make them work in evenly.

Both lid and coffin can now be given a coat of raw linseed oil, well rubbed in with old linen rags, afterwards rubbing off all the surplus oil. The top edges and the under side of the lid where planed may also be oiled, after which the nailing can be proceeded with.

Place the points of the nails in the marks made by the compasses, drive in the outer rows, and fol low with the inner lines, regulating by the eye the distance between the nails, which can be placed either immediately opposite the outer ones, as in the horizontal row, or diagonally with them, as in the vertical rows in Fig. 21. The latter looks the best, as it does not show so plainly any little irregularity in spacing.

The nailing finished, the furniture can be put on, the coffin under consideration having usually three handles each side and one at the head and foot, making eight in all.

The next thing is to pitch the coffin, and this should be done thoroughly, taking care that every crevice and joint is covered, and also that the handle fastenings are well covered.

The holes for screws should now be made. It will have been found that the two screw holes already made came just in the place of nails, and they may now be enlarged and proper coffin screws inserted; and a nail should be withdrawn at each side opposite these two, and screws inserted also. There are now four screws in, two near the head and two at the foot. Two more are required in the sides, at equal distances apart, in each case taking the places of nails, and, the screw-heads matching the nails, the whole presents a uniform appearance.

Care should be taken to bore the holes in the coffin sides large enough for the screws to be driven home without the use of much force, as the heads are liable to fly off; at the same time, they must be tight enough to have a good hold.

In seme districts it is customary to make coffins fish-tailed, the narrowest part being about a foot nearer the breast.

To set out the bottom, proceed in the same way as for the parallel coffin (see Fig. 8, p. 14), and then mark another line across 8 in. from the foot. The head will be 8 in. wide; the width of breast as required; the foot 8 in., and the line above the foot 7 in. Drive in nails at these four points, and strike round by means of a thin rod as before (see p. 15), pressing the rod against a straightedge, in order to obtain the straight part between the breast and foot curves.

Fig. 22 shows a bottom set out as above, and Fig. 23 a somewhat easier method. In the latter, four marks only are required, and the rod is bent round inside the first and third and outside the second and fourth nails, and the pencil run round at once, a straightedge not being required, as there are no straight parts. A little care is necessary in order to get the long curve alike on both sides, as it is easy for it to vary with the pressure of the pencil against the rod; but if the precaution is taken to measure from the centre line to the rod at certain points, they should come nearly correct, but a small difference in the curve has a most noticeable effect in the finished coffin.

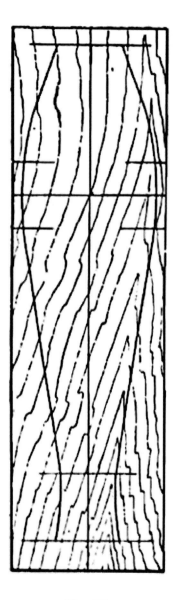

Fig. 22.

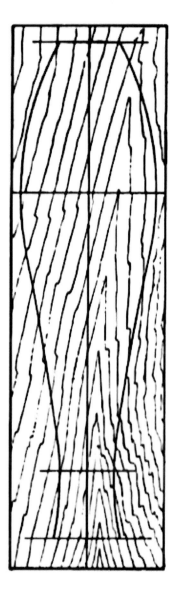

Fig. 23.

Figs. 22 and 23.—Fish-tailed Coffins.

Figs. 24 and 25 show the shapes of two other kinds, both at one time fashionable, and which it is believed emanate from America. They are not handsome; and doubtless the shapes were suggested by the convenience of making them in framed panel work. The method of setting these out will be obvious.

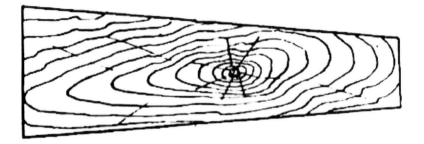

Fig. 24.

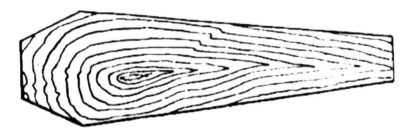

Fig. 25.

Figs. 24 and 25.—American Patterns of Coffins.

CHAPTER III

CHILDREN'S COFFINS; ADULTS' COVERED COFFINS

IN districts where the parallel coffin is in vogue, it is usual to make coffins for children in the same way as for adults; but as there is practically as much work in a small one as in one of full size, the only reduction in cost is owing to the smaller quantity of timber required and the smaller-sized furniture.

The child's coffin to be now described is of the tapered variety, which should be adopted in all cases for the sake of cheapness. It is made in the same way as usual, to the size required, but the wood need not be planed as it will be covered, and hard wood should not be used on account of the difficulty of driving in the necessary tacks. It is not meant that deal should be used, as this will not bend safely; but some kind of soft English wood such as alder, aspen, or something similar, which, being plentiful and practically useless for ordinary work, can be purchased cheaply. Wood 3/8 in. in thickness will suffice for coffins up to 2 ft. 6 in. long; it should be 1/2 in. thick for coffins from 2 ft. 6 in to 4 ft., and above that 3/4-in. should be used.

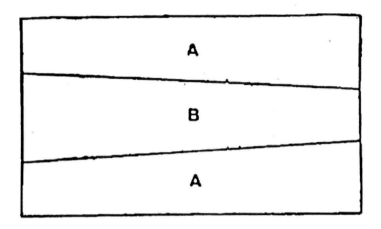

Fig. 26.—Cutting Material for Covering Coffin.

The coffin, having been made and cleaned off level everywhere, must next be pitched and then covered with blue dress material without pattern. By cutting the material as shown in Fig. 26, the three pieces required can be cut out of one length without waste, provided the coffin is not too large, the two pieces marked A being for the sides, and the middle piece B for the lid; but if the material is not sufficiently wide to cut the three pieces easily, it is best to cut only the side pieces out of one length, as Fig. 27, and the piece for the lid out of a separate length. In either case the material should be cut off long enough to reach across the head and along one side of the coffin and about 2 in. over.

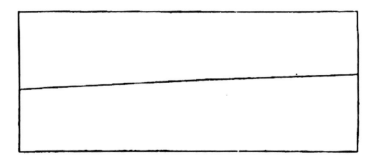

Fig. 27.—Cutting Material for Covering Coffin.

To cover a coffin neatly and quickly requires a certain amount of knack. The best way to begin (see Fig. 28) is by tacking one edge of the covering material along inside the upper edge of the coffin sides, as at C, keeping the tacks well down from the top edge, so as to be clear of the lining tacks, and leaving enough at one end, as at D, to reach across and just turn the opposite corner. When the whole length of the side is tacked, stretch it over outside, tack the material to the bottom, so that the side shows without a wrinkle, then stretch it round across the end, and tack it to the opposite side. It must then be folded over the top edge and tacked inside at the end, cutting the corner so that it can be folded under to form a mitre. Treat the bottom in the same way.

Covering the other side will be a repetition, but it is more difficult, as the ends have to be folded in, and should finish about 1/4 in. from the corner, as shown at E (Fig. 28). The top corners are the most troublesome, and it requires some practice to make a neat job of them.

The coffin has now to be ornamented with stamped white metal, which ranges from 1 1/4 in. to 2 in. in width, made so that it can either be used full width or cut down through the centre; it is obtainable in a variety of patterns, one which looks very well being shown in Fig. 29. This will be wide enough if cut down the middle, unless the coffin is comparatively large, or a "smart" one is desired. The best way to cut it is to place several lengths together, and with a sharp chisel cut through all at once It can then be tacked on round the sides, ends, and lid of coffin, using very short round-headed tacks, keeping it just clear of the edges everywhere, so that the coffin can be handled without displacing it. Corners should be mitred and straight joints lapped. At The ends the ornament should be regulated so that the mitre will cut through the same part of the pattern at each end, as shown in Fig. 30, which represents one end of a finished coffin.

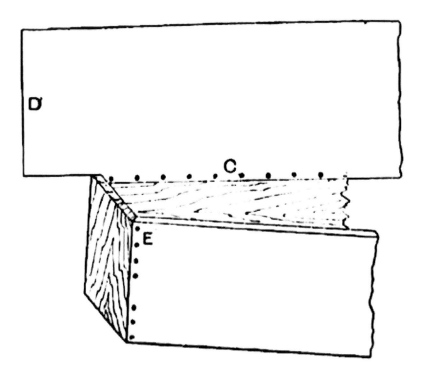

Fig. 28.—Method of Covering Coffin.

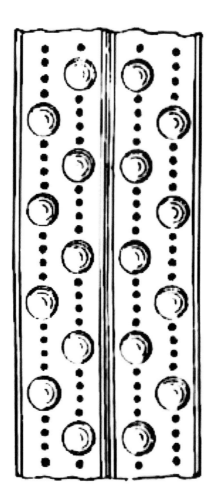

Fig. 29.—white-metal Ornament for Child's Coffin.

The plates and handles will be put on midway between the ornament at top and bottom, using three on each side, unless the coffin is very small, when two will suffice. The lid will be covered in the same way, but more care will be required at the corners. The fold of the material should come exactly at the corner of the lid, so that it will not be seen. In ornamenting the top of the lid, the metal must be coaxed round the bend, for which purpose a full length should be selected, so as to avoid a join on the curved part.

Fig. 30.—Finished End of Child's Coffin.

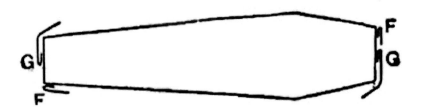

Fig. 31.—Method of Covering Adult's Coffin.

This coffin will be lined in the same way as any other, and by any of the methods which will be described, but care will be needed to prevent the metal ornament getting damaged, as the least touch will displace it; and when this is once done, it is impossible to remedy it.

Sometimes an adult's coffin has to be covered with black cloth, and on rare occasions with more valuable material, such as velvet, etc. If the coffin is to be nailed, the finish of the cloth can be as shown at F in Fig. 31, so that the outside rows of nails will keep the cloth in place, and cause the join to show comparatively little; the tacks which fix the cloth should also be so placed that the nails will cover them. Another method is to bring the joins as shown at G (Fig. 31) in the middle of the head and foot, in which the handle-plate will cover the greater portion of the fold; while the nails at top and bottom can be made to come on the fold and cover the tacks, as before.

The last-named method applies to cases where it is necessary to have two joins in the covering material. If it is narrow, or there are enough covered coffins wanted to allow of a length being cut off to reach completely round, there will then be one join only, and this may be arranged at the centre of the head. In the latter case, the covering material must be allowed wider, so that the sides can be at right angles to the foot, as shown in Fig. 32, the dotted lines showing the coffin, and the solid lines the covering. If this is not done, there will be too much cloth at the bottom of the coffin at the foot end, on account of the latter spreading out at the top. The reason for having the join at the head is that the head is the part least seen; consequently, the join will be less noticeable than if at the foot.

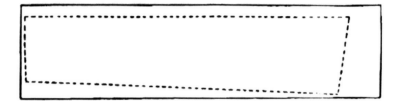

Fig. 32.—Arranging Material for Covering.

To set out for the rows of nails on a covered coffin the lines should be put on the cloth with a fine chalk line; and for the distance between the nails, the compasses can be used as before, the cloth showing the impression sufficiently for the purpose.

Another method of making a black coffin is to proceed in the ordinary way until ready for oiling or polishing, and then to black it over with a dead-black solution, made from vegetable black mixed with turpentine, adding a small quantity of gold size. This dries as fast as put on, and the only difficulty is in finding the exact quantity of the size to use, as if too much is added it will give the surface a glossy appearance, while if too little, the black will rub off; the happy medium can only be found by experiment.

The gauge lines for guides in nailing must be made before blacking, and great care is required in lining a black coffin, or the lining will be discoloured. On the whole, the blacked coffin is not to be recommended; but it has to be made sometimes, when a black coffin is wanted and a cloth cover would be too expensive.

The letter references in Figs. 26, 28, and 31 are explained as follows:—A, covering for side of coffin; B, covering for lid; c, covering material tacked inside coffin; D, part of material to cover head (or foot); E, method of finishing the covering of coffin; F, proper place to finish adult's covered coffin, when ornamental nails are used; G, alternative method, most suitable if nails are not used.

CHAPTER IV

POLISHING COFFINS

THE polishing of a coffin is often left alone by undertakers, under the impression that it cannot be done properly except by an experienced polisher. This is perfectly true as regards polishing in general, but in a coffin the lasting quality of the polish is immaterial. If a good polish to last a few days is obtained, it is enough; and as this can easily be done with a little practice, there is no reason why undertakers should not do the work themselves, instead of sending for a polisher.

French polish can be bought ready prepared, but there is none to beat that made by dissolving 1 1/2 oz. of shellac in a pint of spirits of wine. The shellac should be placed in a bottle, the spirits of wine poured over it, and the whole allowed to stand in a warm place, when, if shaken occasionally, it will quickly dissolve. When dissolved, it can be strained through fine muslin, and is ready for use.

The coffin having been brought to a smooth face with scraper and glasspaper, the pores of the wood must be filled up. If the coffin is of pitch pine, sprinkle dry yellow ochre over it, pour on some raw linseed oil, and with rags, or a bunch of shavings, rub the mixture well in. Yellow ochre can also be used as a filler for oak if a light colour is wanted, but if a dark brown is desired, use dry burnt umber, which produces a rich appearance when polished. The same should be used for elm, which requires a great amount of filling up, being very open-grained; but the result will amply repay any extra pains taken at this stage. The filling accomplished, every particle of dust, etc., must be rubbed off the surface of the wood, a good material for the final rub off being the shavings taken off by the scraper. All nail holes must be stopped with tinted putty, coloured to match the wood, or with stopping composed of beeswax and resin melted together, tinted as required by the addition of a pigment. To use this, a little can be melted on an old tin plate, and a drop taken on a small chisel and dropped into the hole to be stopped. It will harden instantly, and the surplus can be pared off with a chisel, and a final smoothing given with a piece of worn glasspaper.

The coffin can then be bodied in with polish. Take a wad of cotton wool, about the size of an orange, and lay it in the centre of a piece of washed calico, then gather up the corners to make a pad. The wool is soaked with polish, and a touch of raw linseed oil put on the face of the calico. The rubber is now passed lightly over the wood in circular strokes, particular care being taken of the corners and edges. Work the rubber tolerably dry before replenishing it with polish. Give the whole of the coffin a slight coat only at first, and when this is dry go over the whole again with a very thin even coat of polish applied with a camel-hair brush. While this is drying the lid can be bodied in, and by the time this is accomplished the coffin will be dry and ready for finishing off. This is done with the rubber, using very little polish, and it will be as well if the work is rubbed down with a piece of well-worn glasspaper. It will be now found that the surface comes up with a fine polish, the previous coats preventing the final one from sinking in any further.

When a sufficiently fine surface has been obtained and has been allowed to dry fairly hard, it must be gone over again with the rubber very lightly charged with polish, but with a few drops of spirit applied to the face instead of oil. This must be done quickly and with a light touch, as if the rubber is allowed to rest an instant the polish will come off and the appearance of the work be spoiled. The "spiriting off," however, should on no account be omitted, or the polish will go dull on account of the oil left on the surface, which it is the purpose of the spirit to remove or neutralise. If the above instructions are followed closely, and the precaution taken to have the room in which the polishing is done kept warm and free from dust, good results should ensue; but it is impossible to polish a coffin in a damp room.

If wanted quickly, and there is no time to French polish it, the coffin should be stopped and filled as before directed, and then sized over. In a few minutes this will be dry, and can then be rubbed down lightly, and the coffin varnished with good spirit varnish or brush polish. This should be put on quickly with a camel-hair brush, using it freely, and spreading it evenly. If used too sparingly, the work will be streaky; while if not put on evenly, it will run, and dry in waves and ridges. There is a happy knack of putting on just the right quantity in just the right way, which only experience can teach, and, if this is hit upon, the result is not at all bad, though inferior to that secured with French polish.

CHAPTER V

INSCRIPTION PLATES AND COFFIN FURNITURE

THE writing of the inscription plate is generally deputed to an outside tradesman, but is an exceedingly simple matter if set about in the right way. The proper tools to use are fine, short-haired sable pencils, technically known as "writers"; and the letters are written with gold size, and coated with deep gold bronze powder before they are dry. The correct time to apply the powder can easily be found by practice, and in applying it it is best to put on a good quantity, returning the surplus to the bottle after the inscription is finished. The plate may then be rubbed over with an old silk handkerchief to remove any scattered particles of powder which may remain.

The proper shapes of the various styles of letters used in inscriptions can be soon learned by observation, and if a few specimens of type are obtained they will be found of great assistance. There is plenty of variety to be obtained from the various styles of block, Roman, and italic letters, without having recourse to ornamental alphabets, which, indeed, are out of character. Old English is admissible, but only if it can be written correctly.

Figs. 33 to 36 illustrate inscriptions on plates of the various shapes which will be met with in black coffin furniture, but it must be understood that these are not the shapes of the plates themselves, but of the space left plain on the plates for the inscriptions.

Fig. 33 is wholly in block letter. This is a very good style for the learner, as it is easy to alter if the correct outline is not hit upon at first, but the different lines must be written in different sizes, in order to give a well-balanced effect. In this diagram, the words "died" and "aged" are written larger than the remainder of the inscription; but, although it is the style usually adopted in Lancashire, it is decidedly wrong. If these words were reduced to about half size, and the letters forming the name increased by half, the arrangement would be a better one.

The centering or balancing of the lines must be regulated by first lightly pencilling the letters, it being then easy to get them properly balanced. Stops should not be employed at the ends of the lines, but after initials or abbreviations full-stops should be inserted.

B. A. BUCKS

DIED

JAN. 1ST 1900

AGED

21 YEARS

Fig. 33.

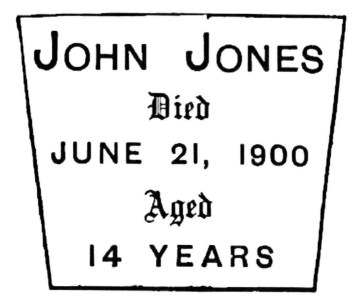

Fig. 34.

Figs. 33 and 34.—Coffin Plates.

Fig. 35 is correctly arranged as far as the styles of type are concerned, but the top line should, if possible, be made a trifle longer, and the second one shorter, so that no two lines are the same length.

Fig. 34 is correctly arranged, with the exception that "died" might be slightly closer to the top line, and "aged" might be a trifle higher.

Fig. 36 shows the best way of arranging the inscription on a heart-shaped tablet, but if the name is a fairly long one it should be arranged in two lines, which will cause "aged" and "years" to come nearly down into the angle, in which case the age must be put in the triangular space above them.

It will often be found necessary to occupy two lines with the name, as initials only are but seldom used. In such cases, if the Christian name is a double one, it should be given a full line to itself, the surname occupying a shorter line beneath it. The latter, however, should form a longer line than the "died," as two short lines together do not look well, and should always be avoided if possible.

On white furniture, such as is used for children's coffins, it is best, for common work, to write the inscription in black; but in better-class work it may be written in gold, and shaded with blue, which looks very well, especially if the coffin is covered with blue material.

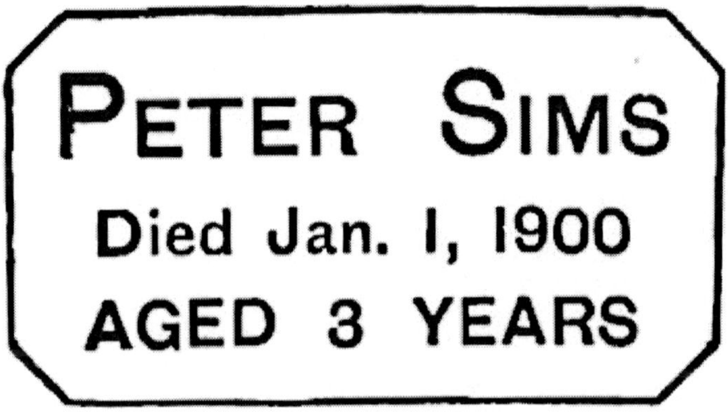

PETER SIMS
Died Jan. I, 1900
AGED 3 YEARS

Fig. 35.—Coffin Plate.

Brass plates should always be engraved, but it is only in

60

large towns as a rule that anyone can be found to execute the engraving. If, by reason of circumstances allowing no other alternative, a brass plate has to be written, the inscription must be executed in black. A good paint for the purpose, which will dry with a gloss, can be made by adding some good varnish to ordinary black paint; and as it would spoil the polish of a plate to pencil the inscription on it, to ensure the lines being properly balanced cut a piece of thin paper to the shape of the tablet, and on this mark out the inscription with pencil, and, when correct, lay it on the plate, with a piece of black transfer paper under it, and mark the outline of the letters with a stylus. This transfers the letters to the plate, and they can be filled in without any trouble.

The shapes in which brass plates are commonly made are shown by Figs. 37 to 40; Fig. 37 is fairly well balanced.

Fig. 40 is correct, the bottom line being condensed so as to make it shorter than the one above. This plate should not be used when the Christian name is long and the surname short.

Fig. 36.

Fig. 37.

Figs. 36 and 37.—Coffin Plates.

The engraving of coffin plates is fully described in a "Work" Handbook, "Engraving Metals," obtainable from the publishers of this present work.

Various kinds of coffin furniture and the methods of fixing will now be considered. Coffin furniture is made in six sizes, known as "infant's," "child's," "boy's," "youth's," "women's," and "men's." The first three can be had in white, white and black, and black and gold, and the second three in black, black and white, and black and gold. All sizes are also made with certain parts enamelled in conjunction with any of the above combinations. This applies to "registered" furniture only, a title given to the better class of stamped goods, the cheaper class being termed "common" furniture. The cheaper variety is made in one or two patterns only, and is plain white or black as the case may be, whilst the "registered" furniture is made in an endless variety of patterns, and has certain parts a dead black, in addition to the foregoing variations. It is, however, in the handles and methods of fixing them that the greatest difference is found between the "common" furniture and the "registered."

Fig. 38.

Fig. 39.

Figs. 38 and 39.—Coffin Plates.

In Fig. 41 is shown a part section of a coffin side with the nipple which holds the handle inserted at A, and at B the ends are shown clenched inside. These nipples are formed by bending the ends of a piece of flat iron together, and swelling it out at the bend to form a loop to take the end of the handle as shown.

The plates are not pierced in any way when bought, so that the holes for the shanks of the nipples have to be made through them at the same time as in the wood, a handle being laid on to get the correct position; the plates are, of course, fixed first with round-head coffin pins made for the purpose. The handles, in the very cheapest sets, are made from bent wire, but in the better ones they are made of cast-iron, either plain or with a slight pattern on the front. The nipples in the registered furniture are cast as shown in Fig. 42, the part in which the handle fits being a, round ball, of about 3/4 in. diameter, with a hole in one side about 1/4 in. deep, and a shank about 3/8 in. in diameter. In this shank are fixed two malleable tangs as shown, for clenching as before. The handle plates are pierced with holes to fit the shanks of the nipples; therefore, after the plates are nailed on, the wood is bored out to the depth required, with a centrebit of the proper size, and continued through with a gimlet for the tang. The handles are of varied designs, and more or less massive, but all are formed with a shank to fit in the holes in the nipples, as shown in Fig. 43.

Fig. 40.—Coffin Plates.

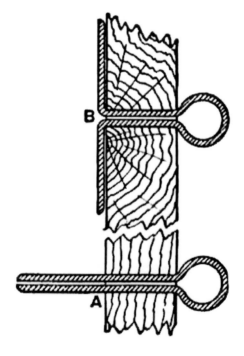

Fig. 41.—Common Handles with Clenched Tangs.

Fig. 42.—Nipple of "Registered" Handles.

Fig. 43.—Stud on Handle to Fit Nipple.

Figs. 44 and 45 illustrate the first attempt to improve upon the old-fashioned registered furniture. The handles were cast with the nipples towards one another, as shown in the latter figure, and an ornamental centre piece secured them, fixed with a common wood screw in the centre, as shown in Fig. 44. The disadvantage of coffin handles supported by a single screw passed through a hollow cap is readily apparent; and the pattern shown by Figs. 46 and 47 is much to be preferred. This is somewhat similar to the former, but, instead of the cap being fixed with a screw, it has malleable tangs cast on at top and bottom, which, passing through the side as shown, are clenched, one upward and downward inside, making them very secure. The handles also, instead of being cast with two nipples, are as shown in Fig. 47, which adds strength. The handle plates are pierced with holes as required for screws and tangs respectively, so that it is impossible to put them on wrong after the plates are fixed.

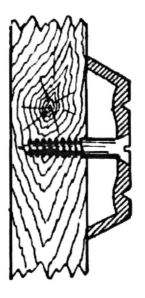

Fig. 44.

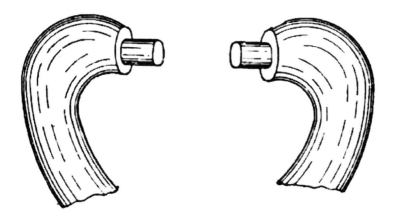

Fig. 45.

Figs. 44 and 45.—Improved Handles.

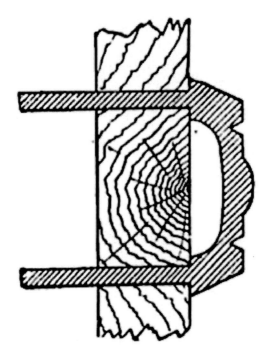

Fig. 46.—Best Form of Handle.

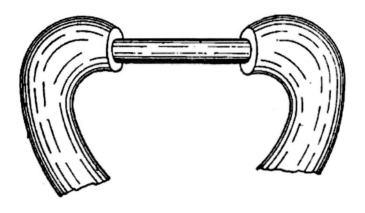

Fig. 47.—Best Form of Handle.

Both of these methods of fixing the handles apply also to brass furniture; but on account of the brass handle plates requiring no fixing in themselves—being made of stouter plate—more care is required in order to get the handles fixed in the exact spot, as they will fix the plate also.

Furniture, except the common variety, should be purchased in sets consisting of breast-plate, lid ornaments, and four pairs of handles and plates, or three pairs of the latter and two pairs of rings, according to the style of coffin usual to the district. The common furniture is best purchased separately, say a dozen breast-plates, with lid ornaments to match, and so many dozen pairs of handle plates and handles; it will then be convenient to use any number of handles on a coffin—according to price—and no sets will be spoiled. The designs of coffin furniture illustrated herewith are taken from the catalogue of Messrs. Dottridge Bros., of East Road, City Road, London, N., and comprise only a few typical examples showing various styles.

Fig. 48.—Common Furniture.

Fig. 48 illustrates the various pieces forming a set of common furniture, two different patterns of lid ornaments and handle plates being given. Figs. 49 and 50 show patterns of "registered" furniture, Fig. 50 being especially good; Figs. 51 and 52 are examples of brass furniture. Some sets have corner clips in addition to the usual ornaments, and if these are used (eight are required) they are fixed to the corners of the coffin so as to give it the appearance of being bound together with brass plates; they are not often used, but look very well

74

with a good set of furniture. Fig. 52 is an excellent set; the handles are very massive, and are suited for a large coffin.

Fig. 49.—Stamped Registered Furniture.

Fig. 50.—Stamped "Registered" Furniture.

Plated furniture, although supposed to be silver-plated, is in reality nickel-plated. If used, a design should be selected in which the handles have a massive appearance and the handle plates are cast, in preference to those made from sheet metal, as the latter have too much the appearance of stamped tin-plate. This can easily be arranged, as it is reasonable to think that, if plated furniture is required, the price of a good set will be no obstacle. "Common" furniture ranges in price from about 1s. 7d. to 2s. 6d. per set for adults, the smaller sizes being slightly less in price. "Registered" furniture costs from 3s. upwards. Brass ranges from 9s. to £4 10s. per set; brass-plated furniture can be had at about 5s.; and if nickel-plated, the cost will be from about 6s. per set.

Fig. 51.—Brass "Registered" Furniture.

Fig. 52.—Brass "Registered" Furniture.

Messrs. Dottridge Bros, also engrave inscription plates, and, by following the instructions given in their catalogue, both furniture and inscription can be ordered by telegraph, whilst correctness is guaranteed.

CHAPTER VI

TRIMMING OR LINING COFFINS

ANY fabric, from plain calico up to figured satin, may be used as coffin lining; but it is hardly likely that the latter material will be very often in request, whilst the former has been almost discarded in favour of flannelette, which costs very little more and has a much better appearance. Another material used for lining is swansdown. This has a very "cosy" appearance, but requires care in using, as it shows every mark, and dirt is very hard to remove. For the better class of coffins, flannel is used, but the very best quality is not often required.

Fig. 53.—Cutting Lining for Tapered Coffin.

The southern counties coffin described in Chapter II., being somewhat the simpler to trim, will be dealt with first.

To obtain the length of lining required, measure, inside the coffin, across the head and along one side, and cut off the material about 2 in longer than the measurement obtained; then, with the help of an assistant, double the piece lengthways, as shown in Fig. 53—allowing the fold to be about 1 1/2 in. out of the square at each end—and cut through the fold. The two pieces should now be exactly alike, but about 3 in. wider at one end than the other, so as to allow for the difference in depth of coffin at head and foot.

If both faces of the lining are alike, as in calico or flannel, the selvedge of each piece can be placed at the top; otherwise, one selvedge and one cut edge will have to be used.

The worker takes the wide end of one piece of lining, stands at the head of the coffin with the face of the material towards him, doubles it in about 1 1/2 in. across the end, and tacks the edge A as near the top of the head of the coffin B as possible, as shown by Fig. 54, with the fold formed by the turned-in edge close up to the junction of the coffin side and head; he stretches the lining fairly tight across the head, and tacks it in the other corner, following along the side until the other corner is reached, when the surplus material must be turned back so that the fold comes exactly to the corner, as at the starting-point.

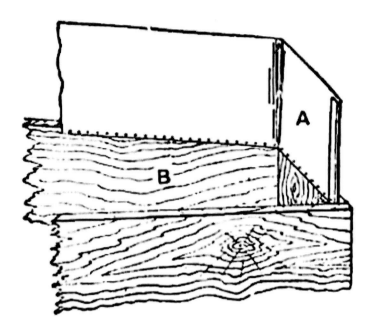

Fig. 54.—Tacking Lining to Coffin Sides.

The other half can now be fixed in a similar manner, but, instead of turning the ends in, nail them round the corners on the turned-in ends of the other length, so that when both are folded down into the coffin the turned-in ends of the first piece will fit down the corners, whilst the ends of the last piece put in (which will be the first to be folded down) will turn the corner and effectually prevent the wood from being seen at the junction.

Tacks should be freely used in putting in the lining, at not more than 2-in. intervals, and they should be put in as close as

81

possible to the top, but not so close as to split the wood.

In a coffin of the cheapest variety the lining would now be finished, as the material is not fixed at the bottom at all, being turned up while the sawdust, or whatever is used, is put in the bottom. By this means the lining is kept free from dust. If the two pieces of lining do not quite cover the bottom of coffin, a loose piece of material can be laid in, and the side linings folded down on it.

A pillow is usually made from the same material as the lining; a pattern for it is first cut in a piece of brown paper to fit in the head of the coffin, and a piece of the lining material folded and cut to the pattern, 1 in. larger all round. The ends and side of the pillow are then sewn up, first filling it with sawdust.

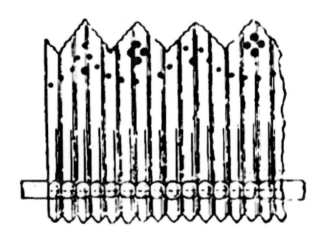

Fig. 55.—Frill.

In a coffin better than the cheapest kind it is usual to pad round the top or tack in a frill, as shown in Fig. 55. Frilling is sold in lengths sufficient for a coffin, in a variety of patterns and of various materials. It is crimped and perforated; and along the back, near the bottom edge, is a piece of tape fixed to the frill; the tape holds the frill in shape and provides a means of attaching it to the coffin, as, by folding the top part of the tape towards the bottom and lifting up the bottom of the frill, tacks can be put in through the two thicknesses of tape close to the top of the coffin. The bottom of the frill will spring down and cover the tacks, and the top part, when pressed forward, forms a fringe round top of coffin. The frill should be fixed close to the top, so that the lining does not show above it, or it spoils the effect. Padding is sometimes used in conjunction with the frill, but is better dispensed with; but if a frill is not used, then a roll of padding round the top improves the appearance, but, to be effective, it must be kept quite to the top. To make this padding, take a sheet of cotton-wool and cut it into pieces about 6 in. wide; tack these round inside the coffin with about half their width projecting above the coffin sides, and tacked close to the top. The wool can then be folded over inwardly, and secured by a few tacks at the bottom edge. This method gives a good firm roll, which will not work downwards.

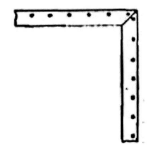

Fig. 56.—Lining Material Mitred at Corner.

Fig. 57.—Alternative Method of Fixing Lining.

Another method of lining a coffin of this style is to tack the lining on the top of the sides as near the outside edge as possible, and then fold it over the tacks so as to cover them. In this case the corners require a little manipulation, and they should be folded so as to form a mitre, as shown in Fig. 56, which also shows the position of tacks, though of course in practice these would be covered by the lining. When the lining is put in by this method, the cotton-wool is put on so as to do away with the sharp corner of the coffin entirely, being brought out to the outside of the boards, and also down inside an inch or two.

The last-mentioned method of lining is not recommended except for a shell, for which it is best adapted if frills are not used; but, unless some particular objection is taken to the frill, it is preferable to use one, and proceed as by the first method, it being more easily and quickly done, and also presenting a better appearance.

The lid of the coffin is lined in all but the cheapest work; a length of lining material as long as the lid and the full width of the stuff should be cut off, folded in about an inch at each end, and tacked to the middle of the lid at the ends, keeping the material to one side so that there will be waste at one side only. It is then cut all round to the shape and size of the lid, and about an inch at the breast is folded in and tacked down, and the same immediately opposite, stretching it fairly tight meanwhile. The four corners are then done, folding them in each way so that an inch margin is shown all round the lid; then a tack is put in at each side, midway between the head and breast, also between breast and foot, and so continued, one tack at each side opposite one another, and midway between those already in, until it is tacked sufficiently. As the tacks will show, they should be evenly distanced, and also kept at equal distances from the edges.

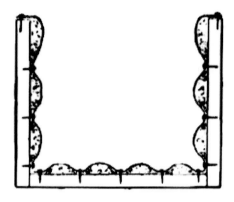

Fig. 58.—Cross Section of Upholstered Coffin.

In lining the Lancashire coffin described in Chapter II., the same material is used, but the material is cut into four pieces: two for the sides about 14 in wide, and two the length for head and foot respectively, of the same width. These four pieces are nailed to the coffin sides in the manner shown by Fig. 57, nailing them inside at the bottom, and folding each piece at the corners to form a mitre, as in Fig. 56.

A piece of the lining is then stretched over and temporarily tacked to the top of the coffin, so that it can be cut roughly to shape. The tacks are then withdrawn, and this piece, which forms the bottom lining, is tacked in, first putting in the sawdust or whatever is to be used in the bottom. In some cases this is put in so thickly at the head that the pillow may be dispensed with, but this is not a good plan; it is far better to cover the bottom lightly all over, and provide a separate pillow in the usual way.

86

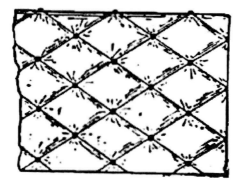

Fig. 59.—Quilting of Padded Lining.

This only applies to the cheaper coffins. The better kind are upholstered, some at the top only as before described, but usually as shown by Fig. 58, which is a cross section of a padded coffin. For this, the lining is cut and tacked on as described above, the coffin turned on its side, and the padding—which is usually cotton-flock—spread evenly over the side as it lies; the lining is then turned in and tacked to the bottom, or to the side as close to the bottom as possible. Fig. 59 shows how the tacks are driven in, the drawing in of the lining at those points gives the effect of upholstering. One side being finished, the coffin is turned over and the other treated in the same manner, also the ends and bottom, taking care not to use the padding too generously, or the depth of coffin may be reduced too much.

The tacks put in to form the quilting are also useful in preventing the padding from being misplaced, a likely occurrence if it is not fixed in any way; and upon the class of work in hand will depend whether they are simply put in so as to show a rough form of quilting only, or whether pains are taken to make a good job, in which case the ordinary tack can be hidden by a covered one to imitate an upholsterer's button. This will be requisite for a high-class coffin, lined with best material.

The lid can be lined in the same way as the former one, but it is more difficult to do on account of the rim being in the way. The better plan when the lid has to be lined is to do it before the rim is put on, bevelling off the edge of the lid on the underside for about half the thickness, and pulling the lining over and nailing it to the bevel thus formed; then, when the rim is nailed on, all the tacks which hold the lining are hidden, and the rim will fit close at the top where it is seen.

In cases where the lid has to be padded as well as lined, it will be done in the same manner as the padding of the coffin.

The side linings of the coffin must be cut and tacked down in the slots in which the cross pieces (Fig. 12, p. 18) fit, and if the lining is snipped on each side of them, the loose piece thus formed can be turned in and a couple of tacks will neatly secure them, so that the fit of the cross pieces will not be interfered with.

Some other additions are often made to the trimming of a Lancashire coffin to take the place of the frill in the southern one, as far as giving it a finish is concerned.

With padded coffins it is customary to use what are called sheets and side strips, made of various materials and stamped and embroidered in various patterns. They are fixed with pins to the lining so that the ornamented edges just meet down the centre of the coffin. The side strips are then—the wrong side up and the ornamented edge inwards—pinned evenly along the whole length and then turned over, so that the pins are covered and the edges droop over the coffin sides.

This is an easy way of making a coffin look considerably smarter with little trouble; but the frilling as previously described looks equally well.

On the day of the funeral the side strips are turned inside the coffin before the lid is screwed on. There are other methods of lining or trimming coffins, but those here detailed should be sufficient to meet all requirements.

CHAPTER VII

ORNAMENTED AND PANELLED COFFINS

HITHERTO only coffins of the cheaper kind have been dealt with, and a few hints as to how their appearance may be improved without in any way affecting their construction will now be given.

One method of giving a little variety to the lid is to put a line of black stamped metal (technically termed "lace"), as shown in Fig. 29, p. 32. round the lid between the rim and the bead. If this is done, the bead must be put on so that the "lace" just fills the space between it and the rim. Reference was made in Chapter III. to the fragile nature of this material, but that warning will not apply in this instance, as it is protected; at the same time it is quite out of character unless the furniture is black, and should then only be used when some little addition is wanted in order to take off the common appearance or bareness of a coffin. Something similar may be done when brass furniture is used, but instead of the "lace" a row of large square-topped brass nails, placed at about 6-in. intervals, is employed. These have a massive appearance and, being hollow, they are cheap, and thus afford a means of improving the coffin at slight cost.

Fig. 60 is a cross section of a coffin lid in which the rims B are bevelled on both edges and nailed on level with the surface of the lid A, in the centre of which an extra panel C with chamfered edges is planted on, leaving a margin of about 2 in. all round.

Fig. 61 shows a somewhat similar embellishment, but instead of the panel C being nailed directly to the lid A a plinth D is first nailed on, to which the panel is fixed, the edges of which in this case are left square, whilst those of the plinth are chamfered. This gives to the lid a handsome appearance, but Fig. 62 shows an improvement on it. In this case the plinth is higher and its edges are rounded off, so that in conjunction with the panel an ovolo moulding is formed. Care should be taken that the effect of these raised panels is not spoiled by unequal margins being shown, the least difference in the curve of either the plinth or panel being apparent at a glance.

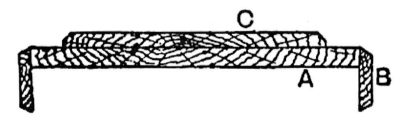

Fig. 60.

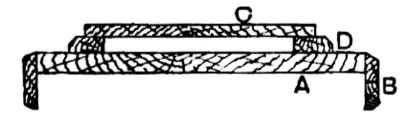

Fig. 61.

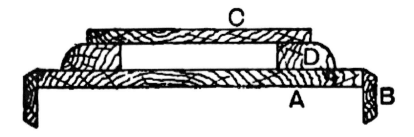

Fig. 62.

Fig. 60.—Section of Lid with Plain Panel.

Figs. 61 and 62.—Sections of Lids with Raised Panels.

In order to ensure the lines of the curves being correct, both plinth and panel can be marked from the lid itself. The plinth should be mitred at the corners, and the sides can be either in one length or of two pieces jointed at the breast, in which case the joints must be made very neatly, and a wooden strip should be put across to support the panel in the middle.

When these panels are used, the margins must be regulated by the size of the inscription plate, as the panel must be wide enough to accommodate it. A good margin improves the appearance, and it should not be under 2 in. even if a smaller plate has to be used; while if the coffin is a wide one a 3-in. margin will not be too much. As a rule, the inscription plate is the only furniture put on the lid, but there is no reason why lid ornaments should not be used as well, if thought desirable. The appearance of a plain lid is improved if the inscription plate is mounted on a piece of wood cut to the exact shape, with the edge either chamfered or rounded off as shown in the section (Fig. 63), E being the plate and F the block.

Fig. 63.—Section of Inscription Plate with Block.

Most of the better class of coffins are panelled. The actual coffin is made in the usual way, in either the parallel or tapered style, and the plinth is put round as before described, except that its edges are left square instead of being chamfered. A similar plinth is then put round near the top, leaving 1/2 in. only, so as to form a rebate of that depth. Short pieces of the plinth are then fixed vertically at each corner, both at the ends and the sides, overlapping them so that a sharp corner is formed; but in order that they may show an even width, the end pieces must be reduced in width by their thickness to allow for the overlapping, as shown by Fig. 64. Two similar pieces are then fixed on each side at right angles to the plinths, so as to divide them into three panels of equal length.

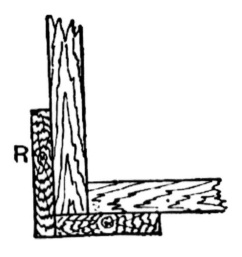

Fig. 64.

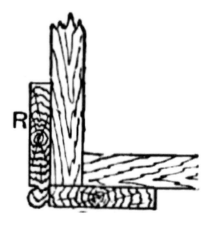

Fig. 65.

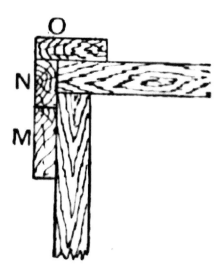

Fig. 66.

Figs. 64 and 65.—Alternative Horizontal Sections of Corner
with Mock Panel Framing.

Fig. 66.—Vertical Section Showing Mock Panelling of Lid.

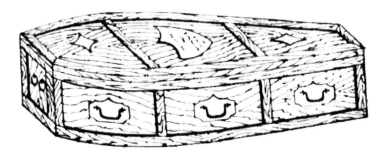

Fig. 67.—Sketch of Panelled Coffin.

Sometimes the corner pieces R on the sides have a return
bead worked on them, as in Fig. 65, instead of being left with

a square corner; and when this is done, instead of reducing the end pieces in width, the side pieces R must be made wider by the size of the bead.

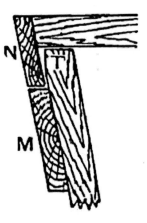

Fig. 68.—Arrangement for Removal of Lid of Tapered Coffin.

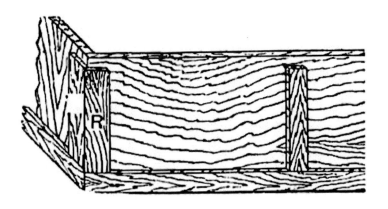

Fig. 69.—Part of Cheaply-made Panelled Coffin.

The lid should now be screwed on, and a rim N (Fig. 66) put round the edge, fitting close to the top plinth M on the coffin. It will project slightly beyond the latter, on account of the extra size of the lid; but the two must be planed off level, and the rim planed off also so as to be level with the top of the lid. A margin O is then fixed round the edge, the side pieces being cut to the required shape, and two cross pieces are then put on so as to divide the lid into three panels to match the sides. Fig. 67 shows a completed coffin in this style.

Fig. 70.—Part Section of Mock Panelled Coffin with Raised Lid.

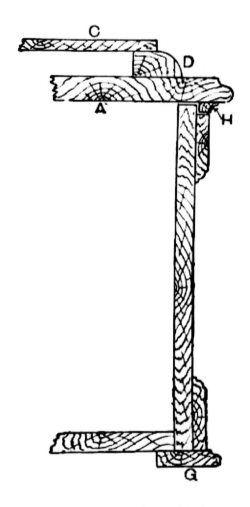

Fig. 71.—Section of Moulded Frame.

When a tapered coffin is panelled by this method, it is necessary to plane off the upper outer edges of the head and foot, as shown at T (Fig. 68), otherwise in fixing the rim, the lid would be fixed to the coffin. The bevelling obviates this, and allows the lid to be lifted off easily.

A cheaper style of panelled coffin, not suitable, however, for good work, is that shown in Fig. 69. It is very similar to the former, but whereas in that shown in Fig. 67 the complete panels are formed on the coffin independently of the lid, in Fig. 68 the panels are completed only when the lid is on, the rim of the latter fitting on to the vertical pieces. The appearance of the mock framing may be improved by working a moulding of some kind on the edges, but this means a considerable increase of work.

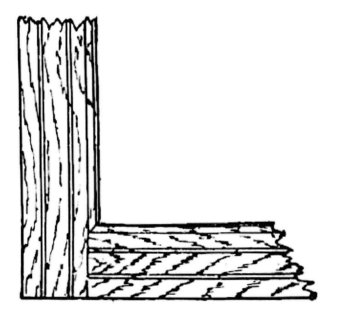

Fig. 72.

Fig. 73.

Figs. 72 and 73.—Alternative Method of Fixing Moulded Framing.

A part section of a handsome coffin is shown in Fig. 70. Its exterior is mock-panelled in the way just described, but instead of the edges of the planted-on framing being square, an ovolo moulding is worked on them and mitred at the joints. A base moulding G is also screwed on round the bottom of coffin, and fixed to project slightly beyond the plinth.

Instead of the lid being provided with a rim, it is made to project 1 in. all round the coffin sides, the edge being moulded as shown, and beneath is fixed a small scotia moulding H, which fits in the rebate formed by the side of the coffin and the top rail of the framing. The lid A is finished with a plinth D and raised panel C just as in Fig. 62, p. 61.

A further embellishment is shown in Fig. 71, which is a section of the planted-on framing with a moulded face, and this can either be fixed with only the edge moulding mitred, the upright pieces at the corners stopping the moulding in the horizontal pieces as in Fig. 72, or it may be mitred the whole width as in Fig. 73; the latter method involves a larger expenditure of labour, whilst the easier method gives as good if not a better effect.

Coming now to the better class of work, in Fig. 74 is shown a portion of a panelled side, the panels being formed in the sides themselves, of which the enlarged section (Fig. 75) will give a better idea by cutting out a moulding as shown, leaving the rectangular panel L intact. It will be evident that these panelled sides can only be made by special machinery; consequently, they will have to be purchased in quantities, and their cost as compared with that of plain sides is considerable. The same effect may be obtained in a cheaper way, which also will possess the advantage that the panels can be arranged according to the length of the coffin, whereas with the stock patterns they will often be out of proportion if used for a short coffin. The panels in each side are three in number, that at the breast being midway between the end ones, and they should be arranged so that there is the same distance between the panels as there is beyond them at each end at the bottom, the bevels of head and foot being ignored in setting out. At the head and foot the width of the panels must be in proportion to the depth of sides, and they should be marked with a straightedge from end to end so that the three panels will be in line, while the ends of the panels should be squared from the bottom edge of the coffin side, not the bottom of the panel.

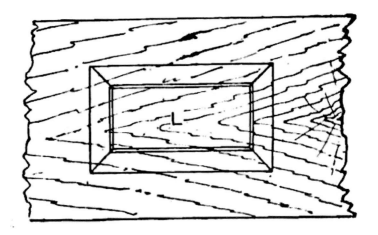

Fig. 74.—Part of Coffin Side with Solid Worked Panel.

Fig. 75.

Fig. 76.

Fig. 77.

Fig 75.—Enlarged Section of Coffin Side with Solid Worked Panel.

Figs. 76 and 77.—Alternative Methods of Fitting Panels.

Having set out the faces of the sides, carefully transfer the lines to the backs, or what will be the insides, then mark round 1/2 in. both inside and outside of the panel lines.

The space between these lines must now be cut away, forming a trench the depth of half the thickness of the side,

105

which can easily be done by boring a series of holes with a centre-bit (taking care to keep the point of the bit inside the panel lines), and cutting away between the holes with a chisel. The trenches can afterwards be cleaned out to the right depth with a router or "old woman's tooth," and it is important that they should be made quite straight and smooth at the bottom, as any inequalities will be apparent when the panels are put in. The trenches finished, with a fine saw cut round the panel lines, and carefully finish the edges with chisel and glasspaper.

The opening for the panel is now left with a rebate 1/2 in. wide all round inside, and in this rebate the panels are fitted and secured by screws, as in Fig. 76, which shows the panels raised, or as in Fig. 77, which shows a plain panel with a small quadrant moulding R tacked round. In the latter case there is no necessity for being very particular about the finish of the bottom of the trench, as the moulding will cover all irregularities; but when the raised panel is used, too much care cannot be taken in this respect.

These home-made sides have advantage over those worked in the solid, as the panels can be better finished, and can also be removed for polishing—a great convenience, as there is some difficulty in getting the polish into the corners.

It is very unlikely that a coffin of this description would be used except in conjunction with a shell; but if otherwise, the panels would have to be thoroughly pitched all round.

The size of the handle-plates must, to a certain extent, regulate the size of the panels, as it is obvious that the plain part of the panel must be large enough to allow a fair margin beyond them; the width and length of the panel should also bear some comparison with the same dimensions of the plates, so that the completed coffin will present a uniform appearance.

It is not usual to panel the head and foot, as it is difficult to secure correct proportions; but if two rings are used, as in the parallel coffins, then it is easy to make a panel look well. If this is decided on, the depth of panel should coincide with those in the sides, and the width be regulated so as to show the same margin at the sides as at top and bottom. The rings should be inserted in the solid part.

A properly framed panelled coffin will now be described. The framing may be put together with mortise and tenon joints—a joiner's method of doing panelling—or it may be dowelled, this method being usual among cabinet makers, and the one which will be adopted in the present instance, as, the muntin at the breast line having to be curved, it would be awkward to cut tenons on it. The coffin should, if possible, be arranged so that the panels in the sides are of equal length, but when the bend occurs at the middle of a muntin, this cannot always be managed. Although not obligatory, it is preferable that the coffin should have upright ends; but whether made with square or bevelled ends, and parallel or taper, the two muntins must be at right angles to the bottom rail, whilst the stiles should always be the full depth of the coffin in length. If the corners are to be left square, both stiles and muntins should be of the same width; but if a return bead, or a chamfer, is formed at the corners, then the stiles should be got out so much wider than the muntins. All this must be arranged when setting out the coffin, as it cannot be altered afterwards.

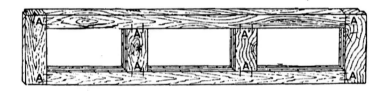

Fig. 78.—Framework of Coffin Side.

A panelled coffin should be made with the sharp curve at the breast only, as, although it is not impossible to make it with the gradual curve, as with a parallel coffin, this would involve a great deal of trouble; therefore, if this latter shape must be worked to, the panel work should be formed as previously described.

Fig. 79.—Section of Curved Muntin.

Fig. 80.—Section of Panel.

The bottom will be got out in the usual way, and all the other stuff must be faced up as for ordinary joinery. If the ends are to be square, and the coffin parallel, the various parts can be set out with square and chisel, as easily as a panelled door; but if tapered, and with bevelled ends, it is best to lay the work out on the bench, and mark where the shoulders come on each piece; the bevels will then be certain to come right. The muntins and rails must be cut off to the marks, and if necessary planed on the ends, and the whole side can be laid out as shown in Fig. 78, each joint being close up, and each part in its proper position. The marks A are then made across each joint as shown, and these are squared across on the edge or end as the case may be, and gauge marks made parallel with the face of the stuff; and at the points where these marks intersect the boring bit is inserted. Four dowels at each joint will be sufficient, arranged in zig-zag order and of about 5/16 in. in diameter, and these can be purchased ready made in long rods. All the dowel holes should be bored before the grooving is done, or it will be difficult to bore them true.

Fig. 81.

Fig. 82.

Figs. 81 and 82.—Alternative Sections of Panels.

The curved muntin must be made from a thicker piece of wood, as shown in section by Fig. 79, the proper curve being obtained by marking from the bottom; the + marks indicate the disposition of the dowels. The saw kerfs for bending the rails must be marked before the dowel holes—which should be kept well away from them—are bored, but not cut until afterwards. The dowel holes having been bored in one side of the ends of the curved muntins, a couple of loose dowels can be inserted in each end and the rails bent round; the marks for the remaining dowels may then be made and the holes bored. The ends of the coffin are treated in the same way as the sides.

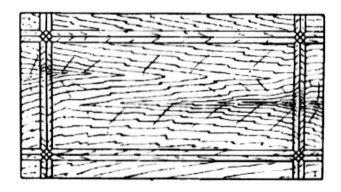

Fig. 83.—Plain Panel with Reeded Ornamentation.

The panels should not be less than 3/4 in. thick, and they may have either a plain or raised face; if plain, they must be mulleted at the back, as shown in Fig. 80. Fig. 81 shows the proper raised panel in section, and an easier method is shown by Fig. 82. The edges should be made a good fit to the grooves, as nothing looks worse than a space between the panel and the framing, and it is a good plan to give them a coat of polish before fixing them. A simple method of ornamenting panels is shown in Fig. 83, consisting of two or more reeds crossing each other, to form Oxford corners; it is best done on a vertical spindle moulding machine, but may be hand-worked without much difficulty, if the precaution is taken to work across the grain first. A section of this beading is shown in Fig. 84, and Fig. 85 shows a simple though less effective ornament, formed with a V-joint plane.

Fig. 84.

Fig. 85.

Figs. 84 and 85.—Sections of Panels.

In putting together, the two bottom rails are first nailed to the coffin bottom, then the dowels driven in slightly, the muntins stuck on to the ends, and the central panels inserted. The dowels are then placed on the top rails, and a coat of good hot thin glue given to the ends of muntins and the dowels, after which the joints can be cramped up tightly and left to dry. While the glue is setting, the ends must be cut to the exact width, the dowels fitted, and the end panels placed in their grooves, and the joints glued up as before. The side stiles are also fitted and glued, and the head and foot can then be placed in the rebates made for them, as shown in Fig. 86, and a short piece of timber placed across each, when, by means of a long cramp, reaching from head to foot, ends and stiles are pulled on at once. It may be necessary to transfer the cramp from the top to the bottom of the coffin—unless two are available—as the stiles must be pulled on nearly parallel, or the dowels will be strained. It is also as well to place a small cramp across the breast, to prevent it being forced outwards; the bottom, being nailed, will be safe. The head and foot can now be nailed to the bottom, and the stiles of sides nailed to those of head and foot. The small holes in the top edges of the sides and ends, formed by the grooves in the stiles, must be filled up by glueing in pieces of wood; and when the glue is dry, the whole can be cleaned off.

Fig. 86.—Stiles of Sides Rebated for Head and Foot.

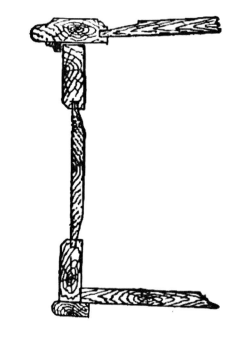

Fig. 87.—Part Vertical Section of Panelled Coffin.

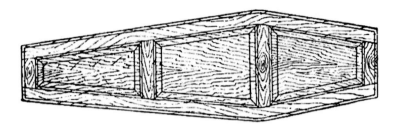

Fig. 88.—Plan of Panelled Lid.

A good effect is obtained by running a moulding, or even a chamfer, on the edges of the framing; if this is done, the moulding must of course be mitred at the joints, and in boring for the dowels a very slight draught can be allowed, so that the mitre will be forced up tightly. Fig. 87 shows a part vertical section of panelled coffin, with the framing chamfered, the panels reeded as in Figs. 83 and 84, and the lid with moulded framing and raised panels. The edge of the lid is moulded, a scotia fillet is planted underneath, and a projecting fillet is nailed round the bottom. Fig. 88 is a plan of the lid with moulded framing and raised panels, for which no detailed instructions are required, it being framed together in the same way as the coffin, due allowance being made for its projection over the sides of the coffin; the moulding round the edge should be worked after the lid is glued up.

It is necessary to mention that a coffin of this style should not be made except in cases where a shell is used; there are too many pieces in it to ensure it being made proof against leakage;

not only so, but in order that the style may be effective, a larger size than that of the ordinary coffin is necessary.

CHAPTER VIII

SHELLS AND OUTER COFFINS

WHEN a shell is ordered, it is made in the same manner as the coffins previously described, and can be either tapered or parallel, according to the style adopted. The wood need not be very carefully selected, as it will be entirely covered; but at the same time it must be as sound as if intended for the coffin proper. It will be pitched, lined, and padded, or trimmed complete, but handles or furniture will not be required; in fact, there is no necessity for the outside to be planed, except for the reason that the shell is usually taken home before the outer coffin. However, as rough, unplaned wood looks bad, it is best to take the roughness off the boards, and give the shell a coat of raw linseed oil.

Before the shell is taken out of the shop it should be laid upon the board selected for the bottom of the outer coffin, when, with a pencil held flat against the side, the outline can be marked so that the bottom will be about 1/8 in. larger all round than the shell; this will ensure the one being a good fit inside the other. Should the shell be of the tapered kind, with bevelled head and foot, the correct bevel of these must also be taken, and also the full depth at both ends—the latter dimension will also have to be taken if the coffin is parallel—and these various measurements should be carefully booked.

If a lead coffin is ordered, the shell should be made in the same way as before, and then covered over with sheet lead. The lead cover should be put on before the shell is either pitched or trimmed, as the cover would be likely to be broken and the shell spoiled. Both the shell and the lid are covered with lead, and full instructions on making lead coffins are given in the next chapter. The lead may finish off level with the top of the sides and ends, or it may turn over and finish inside—the latter plan perhaps being the best. The lid is also covered and turned down so that it will overlap the sides 1/2 in., along which joint the soldering will be done.

Another method is to leave the lead projecting sufficiently above the sides to be level with the lid when it is put on, and it is then covered on the top only, with just sufficient turning down on the edges to enable it to be tacked; and when the lid is dropped in its place, a joint can be wiped round where the lead meets. The latter method has the advantage that there is no need to lift the shell out of the coffin in order to solder it up; but it has the disadvantage that great care is needed to prevent the projecting lead from being damaged during the process of lining and trimming. A preferable way, perhaps, is to have the lead fitted by the latter method, but sufficiently loose to allow the wood shell to be lifted out; all the inside work can then be done, and the lead finally fitted at the last. If a lead coffin is to be used, there is no necessity for planing the wood of the shell anywhere, except at the top edges, which will show until the lid is on, unless they are covered with the lining. The method of striking out the bottom of the outside coffin will apply equally when the shell is covered with lead, providing the outline is marked after the lead is on. Make due allowance for the thickness of the lid of shell, also the bottom of the outside coffin when calculating the width of the sides for the latter; and beyond these measurements allow an extra 1/4 in., the reason of which will be explained later.

The following is an example of calculating the width of sides for outside coffin:—

Depth of shell outside	**12 in.**
Thickness of lid	**1 ,,**
Thickness of bottom for outside coffin	**1 ,,**
Extra	**¼ ,,**
Full width of sides required	**14¼ in.**

A tapered coffin must be calculated in the same way. Particular stress is laid upon the necessity of getting all dimensions correct, as naturally mistakes cause much unpleasantness, and are very difficult to put right.

Fig. 89.—Section of Coffin with Shell and Outer Case.

In Fig. 89 is shown a cross section of a coffin with shell complete, the various parts being: A, shell; B, lining; C, frill; D, body of outside coffin; E, plinth; lid; G, handle-plate and handles.

The coffin will be made in the same way as before described, taking care to get the saw kerfs at the right places, and also to get the bevel of the head and foot correct. Apart from this there is nothing different from making the ordinary coffin, except the plinth. This is put on for the purpose of relieving the broad expanse of plain wood, nails being too

119

common an ornamentation for a good coffin. The lid is chamfered, and as it is impracticable to put a rim round, on account of the bevelled ends, a small fillet H (Fig. 90) can be bradded on to fit close to the coffin. In putting on the furniture, recesses must be cut inside the coffin to clinch the handle fasteners into, so that there are no projections inside to prevent the shell dropping in easily; and for the same reason the outside coffin should not be pitched.

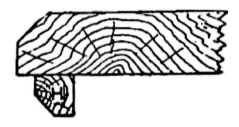

Fig. 90.—Section of Lid with Fillet.

Fig. 91.—Coffin Screw.

The lid of the outside coffin should be fastened on with the kind of screw shown in Fig. 91—that is, if brass furniture is used, which is most probable—but as they are only formed by casting a brass head on a common screw (see the dotted lines), sometimes with very little provocation the head turns round while the screw refuses to move; therefore the holes for the screws should be very carefully bored, so that the screw will bite, yet require no force to get it home. Fig. 92 shows the position of the screws in the coffin lid, and the arrangement of the furniture.

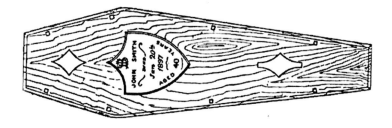

Fig. 92.—Coffin Lid with Screws and Furniture.

In the making of a shell and an outside coffin of the parallel variety the same procedure is followed, except that a rim is put round the lid as usual.

CHAPTER IX

LEAD COFFINS

THE practice of encasing dead bodies in lead extends back to very early times, and there is evidence of this in the ancient lead coffins on view in the museums. All old lead coffins were made of lead cast on wooden frames with sand beds; as there was but little difficulty in printing designs on the sand, many old coffins made of cast lead have raised ornaments on the surface, this conducing to the opinion that they were not intended to be buried underground, but to be placed in vaults or catacombs. Beneath the paving of an ancient church there is a very old lead coffin which is bossed to the rough shape of a human figure, even the shape of the face being roughly outlined.

The so-called lead coffins of the present day consist of wood shells either covered outside or lined inside with milled sheet-lead. The latter kind is rarely made, as the inside lining and trimmings cannot be tacked on without making holes through the lead, and consequently the coffin would not be air-tight.

The sheet lead used varies, according to the class of

work, from ·051 to ·136 of an inch in thickness, or, as usually described, from 3 lb. to 8 lb.—that is, weighing that number of pounds per square foot.

Of the many shapes and forms for coffins, it is not necessary to refer to more than one, as the principles of the plumber's work are the same for all, and need only be varied to suit circumstances.

The most common practice is to cover a deal shell, and after the corpse has been hermetically sealed down, to place the whole inside an oaken coffin. Before starting to cover the shell, it is necessary to cut grooves in it wherever the seams are intended to come, so that the latter may be made perfectly flush on the face with the lead. Fig. 93 shows a section of such dishing, the method of lapping the lead, and the soldering.

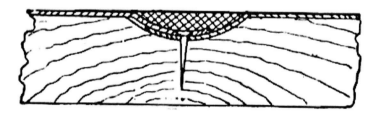

Fig. 93.—Flush-wiped Soldered Seam.

Of the many methods for putting on the lead coverings, the simplest and most economical is to use four pieces—namely, one for the top or lid, one for the bottom, and two for the sides. The latter pieces are made long enough to return half-way across the head and foot respectively, with an extra 1/2 in. for lapping in the seam. The sheet of lead should be unrolled on a clean, even floor, and dressed smooth by means of a flapper made out of a remnant of sheet lead. This does not leave bruises and tool marks as when wooden dressers are used. The shell lid is laid as a pattern on the lead and scribed round with a pair of compasses, having one leg blunted or muffled, set to 3/4 in. The margin is for turning round and nailing to the edges of the lid. The shell is then laid bottom downwards on the sheet, and scribed round with a pointed piece of chalk so as not to scratch the lead. Inside the scribing, parallel lines should be drawn at a distance equal to the outer edge of the groove from the edge of the wood shell, and this will be the exact size and shape of the bottom lead. The groove is shown by dotted lines (Fig. 94). With coffins of certain shapes, the lid can be used as a pattern, and will give the exact size.

Fig. 94.—Wood Shell on Trestles.

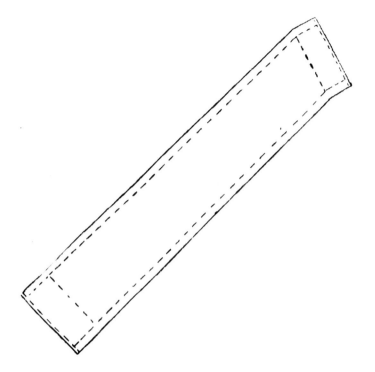

Fig. 95.—Setting Out Lead for Covering Side and Half of Ends.

The side pieces can be set out from measurements taken from the shell, and the shape will be shown by Fig. 95 if the toe is sloping, and if the latter is upright the bottom end will be set out in a line from the side. After cutting out one side, this can be turned over and used as a pattern for the other, but this does not matter much, as the sides can be cut out both alike, and then one of them turned before using. The dotted lines in the figure show the exact size of the shell, and outside these are the margins for dressing round the edges.

Fig. 94 shows the shell supported on a pair of trestles, and the piece of lead for the sides laid on ready for dressing down. After covering one side, the whole is turned over on the trestles, and the other side is treated in the same manner. The shell is then turned with the bottom upwards, the piece of lead that was cut out for it laid on and chased into the groove to lap slightly over the side lead, as shown in the section (Fig. 93), and temporary nails or tacks driven in half-way to hold it in its position.

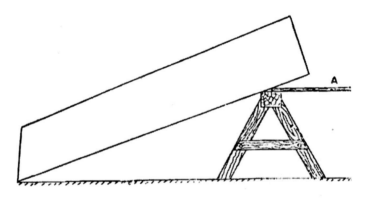

Fig. 96.—Shell in Position for Soldering End Seam.

The sides of all the seams are then soiled or tarnished, or coated with a thin paste made of flour and water and thoroughly dried. The seam is then shaved, an iron straightedge being used as a guide for the shave hook, the temporary nails being removed as the shaving is done, after which permanent nails are driven in as shown by Fig. 93. For good work, copper tacks with tinned heads should be used, but for cheap work with very thin lead, ordinary tinned tacks answer fairly well. After preparing the work thus far, the shell is placed (as shown by Fig. 96) for soldering the end seam, a board A being placed for catching the solder that drops off. The cloth used for wiping the seams should be of a fairly good thickness. Sometimes a small piece of deal lath is placed inside to prevent it bending, which results in the seam being hollow instead of flush. After wiping one end seam, the coffin is reversed, and the other end treated in the same manner. After the ends have been wiped, the coffin is placed on a pair of trestles, so that the bottom is upwards and level, and pieces of board are placed all round near the top edge, for preventing the solder falling on the floor. Some plumbers stick a piece of pasted brown paper on the ends of the end seams where they join the bottom seam, but a good wiper can dispense with such aid.

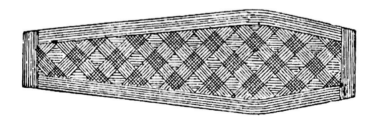

Fig. 97.—Lid After Card-wiring.

While the seams are being wiped, the lead at the sides will

expand by the heat and become uneven. These bumps should be dressed down flat with a flapper made of lead, so as to avoid making any tool marks. The soil or tarnishing material used on the lead should then be washed off with water in which a piece of soda has been dissolved. The piece of lead that was first cut out is then laid on the shell lid and flapped smooth, and the edges dressed down and nailed about 3 in. apart. For getting uniformity of colour, this lead should also be washed.

The whole of the lead (sometimes the bottom is omitted) is now scored with worn scratch- or card-wire. It is an advantage to mount the card-wire on a piece of thin board about 4 in. by 4 in. To give a more finished appearance, the scratches can be laced, similar to a basket work or diaper pattern, or as shown by Fig. 97. The first carding marks should be perfectly straight and parallel from end to end, the lacings being put on afterwards, and the margins done last. A stencil about 18 in. long by 6 in., with a parallel slit in the centre about 2 in. wide, can be made out of a piece of thin wood, sheet lead, or any thin metal, and used for the centre portion, and the fingers can be used against the edge as a guide for the margins.

When coffins are lined with lead, it is usual to cut this to shape in one piece: that is, the bottom, ends, and sides are all joined together. There are several ways of doing this. In Fig. 98 the shape of the bottom is found as has been before described, care being taken that the thickness of the shell side, and also the lead, is allowed for. The sides are measured with a rule, or marked on a rod and transferred to the lead, the setting-out being done with chalk lines, so that the lead is not weakened in the angles by scoring with a hard-pointed tool. By this method the angles, shoulders, and rounded parts at B are prepared and wiped inside as for ordinary cistern or sink linings. If the setting-out is carefully done, the lead can be soiled and shaved when laid flat, before folding for placing in position.

Another method of cutting out the lead is shown by Fig. 99, which is self-explanatory. The outer dotted lines show where the lead folds over the top edges of the coffin, and the narrow strips, also shown by dotted lines, at the angles are for turning up as undercloaks for preventing the solder running through when wiping.

Yet another method is to cut the lead so that the bottom and end are in one piece, and the two sides are separate, but this entails a greater length of soldering.

The most unpleasant part of lead coffin work is the soldering down. It has to be done away from the workshop, and in addition to the lack of working conveniences, such as a fire in the room for melting the solder and heating the irons, the work may have to be done in the presence of the deceased's relatives and friends, and this interferes with the plumber's freedom of action. The shell, too, is usually made to dimensions taken from the body immediately after death, but the latter frequently becomes enlarged, if kept exposed to the air for a few days, and there is some little difficulty in putting on the lid or cover. Although it cannot always be done, in most cases heavy weights on the top of the lid and a rope twitch round the shoulders of the shell will pull the parts together sufficiently for the lead to be soldered up.

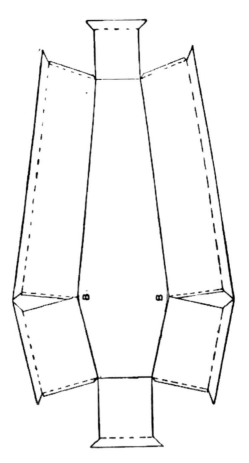

Fig. 98.—Lead for Lining Shell.

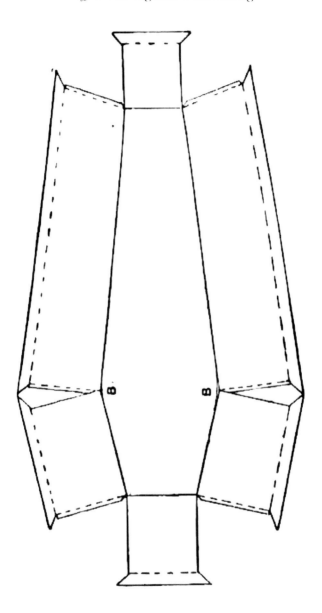

Fig. 99.—Another Method of Cutting Out Lead for Lining Shell.

Fig. 100 is a section of the soldered joints of the lid to the body of the shell, showing the chamfered edges of the woodwork, the treatment of the lead, and the flush soldering. Before the wiping is done, the lead at the sides of the seam is soiled or tarnished, and then shaved as was described for the bottom. Nailing is unnecessary, but sometimes, when the joint is gaping open, pieces of soft paper are caulked in and then covered with narrow strips of lead shaved on both sides and secured in position by little clips raised at the sides and turned over the edges by means of the point of a shavehook or drawing-knife. If the strips of lead have to be wide, they are sometimes secured by a few tinned copper tacks, otherwise they would rise by expanding when heated, and show through the surface of the finished soldering.

Fig. 100.—Section of Soldered Seam Round Lid of Lead-covered Coffin.

When soldering down a lead coffin, the applied heat

causes the air inside to expand, and this expanded air gives the plumber trouble by bubbling through the melted solder when he is wiping. To prevent this, a small hole should be made through the centre of the lid with a large bradawl or a gimlet, to allow vent for the expanded air; and so that the plumber can work in comfort a piece of 1/2-in. or 3/4-in. lead pipe is fitted to the hole and made good temporarily with a putty joint, the other end being carried through the window of the room for conveying any escaping gases out of doors.

There is usually a carpet in the room, and it should be covered with sheets of brown paper and boards fixed round the shell as shown by dotted lines (Fig. 100), for preventing waste of solder and injury to floor coverings. After the seam has been wiped, the smudge or soil should be washed off, and the card-wiring re-done over the solder and disfigured parts.

When sufficient time has elapsed for the air inside the coffin to return to its ordinary density, the vent pipe is removed, and the hole soldered over and carded to match the surroundings. Fig. 101 shows the soldered joint to the lid of a lead-lined coffin, also the outer lid to which the name plate is attached. In screwing on the outer lid, care should be taken when boring the screw-holes not to injure the lead or to make any holes in the lining to allow air to enter. A lead coffin that is not air-tight does not answer its intended purpose of preserving its contents from decay.

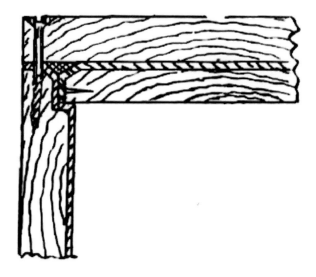

Fig. 101.—Section Showing Soldered Seam and Outer Lid.

CHAPTER X

UNDERTAKING

THE placing of a body in a coffin is a gruesome duty, yet it has to be done. The proper way is to place two strong towels under the body, one near the shoulders and the other just below the waist. The coffin being placed on the bed, the loose material in the bottom is evenly spread, and the lining and pillow adjusted; the body can then be easily lifted in, and need not be further disturbed.

In cases where a shell is used, the best way is to place the outer coffin on the floor, with a piece of wood about 1/8 in. thick placed on the bottom about a foot from each end. Pieces of strong webbing are then placed under the shell at about 9 in. from each end, and long enough to afford a good grip clear above the coffin sides; the shell can then be lowered gradually into the coffin, where it will rest on the two strips of wood, so that the webbing can be withdrawn.

Fig. 102.—Coffin Trestle

When taking a coffin home, it is advisable also to take two small trestles as shown in Fig. 102; they should be about 18 in. high and 21 in. long. Three legs, as shown, are preferable to four, as affording a firmer stand on an uneven floor, but care must be taken to place the coffin exactly over the centre to ensure stability; the trestles should be painted black and be left unvarnished.

On the day of the funeral the undertaker should be punctual, and should lose no time in going through the preliminaries and getting the coffin downstairs. This is often a troublesome matter, especially if the staircase is narrow. A band of strong webbing (Fig. 103) should be provided just large enough to fit easily on the foot of the coffin; it will then slip up about a foot and tighten itself. On two of the sides and opposite one another a piece of the same webbing about a foot in length is sewn to form loops to hold by at the sides.

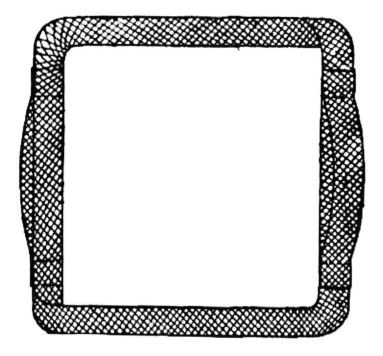

Fig. 103.—Webbing Band.

There are some staircases down which it is almost impossible to get a coffin, and in such cases the only alternative is to get it out of a window. In this case, two planks of similar length are placed against the window-sill, the bottom ends being slightly embedded in the ground or scotched so that they cannot slip, and the top ends as nearly level as possible with the top of the sash bead. Keep the planks far enough apart, so that the coffin will not overhang at the sides, and with a thin rope passed through the handle or rings at the foot and threaded through the side handles the coffin is then lifted on to the planks foot foremost and allowed to slide gently down.

The undertaker should always obtain possession of the burial certificate before starting for the cemetery, as if left behind it may be the cause of an awkward delay. It is quite within his province to supply the necessary hearse and conveyances, and he should also be ready to supply gloves and hatbands in those somewhat rare cases where they may possibly be demanded.

In some places a bier (Fig. 104) is employed as a substitute for a hearse. It can be made from good yellow deal, free from knots and faulty places. The sides A will require to be about 8 ft. long, of 4-in. by 2-in. section, the stretchers B of similar section, 2 ft. long, and the legs C 2 in. square and 21 in. long. The method of construction will be evident from Fig. 104; the stretchers are tenoned into the sides and secured with pins, and the legs secured in the same way. The two end stretchers should be distant 5 ft. 6 in. from outside to outside. This will leave 15 in. at each end to form handles, which should be shaped as shown and rounded smoothly, so that the bier can be carried comfortably either in the hands or resting on the shoulders. The whole should be nicely chamfered for the sake of appearance. In the outer side of each end stretcher is inserted an iron staple D, to which leather straps are fixed so that there is no chance of their being lost. These straps are passed through the head and foot handles of the coffin when the bier is in use. If made with two intermediate stretchers instead of one, as shown, the bier will then be useful for small coffins, but in this case each of the stretchers must be furnished with straps.

Fig. 104.—Hand Bier.

The legs of the bier may also be braced, if desired, but this is undesirable unless it is likely to have rough usage, as every extra piece adds to the weight. The question of weight needs consideration. Oak for the framing would be superior both as regards lasting qualities and appearance, but it is far too heavy; deal is light, and, if straight-grained and given a coat of varnish at intervals, it will be found fairly durable.

Biers may be mounted on wheels, of which either two or four can be used. Figs. 105 to 107 illustrate a two-wheeled bier. The wheels should be lightly made, and of about 3 ft. diameter, and the axle should be about 2 ft. long between the arms. The springs are fixed to the axle by clips E (Fig. 107) and the cross-piece of wood F, and to this cross-piece is fixed the top or framing G, which is made from 3 in. × 2 in. deal or, better still, oak or ash. The outside width of this frame is the same as that of the hand bier, and in length it is the same as the distance between the legs, so that when lifted on the carriage it will just span the frame. In the sides of the framing, four studs H must be fixed, standing above the wood about 1 1/2 in., and corresponding holes should be bored in the sides of the hand bier to fit over the studs to keep it from shifting when in position; these studs and holes should be so disposed, as regards the distance from the ends and sides, that the bier may be interchangeable end for end.

In the centre of the underside of the end cross-pieces of the carriage, eye-bolts or staples must be fixed, to which scotching sticks I are connected. The latter may be either round or octagonal, about 1 1/4 in. in diameter, and long enough to reach within about 2 in. of the ground when the carriage is unloaded. They are fixed to the eye-bolts by means of a staple driven in the end of each stick, and are then free to swing in any direction. When the carriage is being pushed along the road, the scotching sticks should be turned up on to the axle. Scroll springs may be substituted for those shown in Figs. 105 to 107 by discarding the cross-piece F, and making the top frame with three cross-pieces instead of two; the scrolls of the springs will then be screwed direct to the underside of the frame, leaving an equal distance back and front so as to preserve the balance.

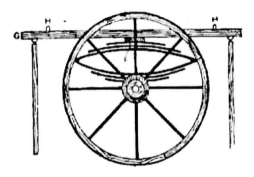

Fig. 105.

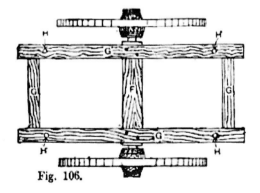

Fig. 106.

Fig. 106.

141

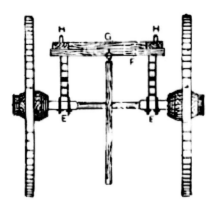

Fig. 107

Figs. 105 to 107.—Side Elevation, Plan, and End Elevation
of Two-wheeled Bier.

With private graves it is in some parts usual to provide
what is termed a "coffin board"; this is a plain board about
1 in. larger all round than the coffin it has to cover, fixed
together with ledges so placed that they rest on the coffin lid
clear of plates or ornaments. Its purpose is that when the grave
is re-opened the board will preserve the coffin from damage,
and it will also form a resting place for the next coffin.

The last point to be touched upon is the question of
infectious diseases. In such cases there is, of course, always a
risk, and it is well to take precautions against infection, such
as staying as short a time as possible in the room, having some
simple disinfectant about the person and on the clothes, and
never undertaking such commissions when fasting, or when
suffering from any other form of exhaustion or depression. If

these simple precautions are observed the risk will be at least minimised.